# *The* SYNAGOGUES *of* CENTRAL AND WESTERN PENNSYLVANIA

## *A Visual Journey*

# The SYNAGOGUES of CENTRAL AND WESTERN PENNSYLVANIA

## A Visual Journey

### Julian H. Preisler

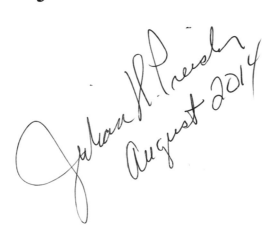

FONTHILL

*Front cover top image*
B'nai Israel Synagogue - Negley Avenue, Pittsburgh,
Pennsylvania. Vintage postcard courtesy of the Rauh
Jewish Archives at the Senator John Heinz History
Center, Pittsburgh

*Front cover bottom image*
Rodef Shalom Synagogue - Fifth Avenue, Pittsburgh,
Pennsylvania. Vintage postcard courtesy of
Congregation Rodef Shalom Archives, Pittsburgh

*Back cover photo*
B'nai Jacob Synagogue - Middletown, Pennsylvania.
Photograph courtesy of Jack E. Kapp of Kapptured
Moments Photography, Philadelphia

Fonthill Media LLC
www.fonthillmedia.com
office@fonthillmedia.com

First published 2014

ISBN 978-1-62545-049-4

Typeset in 10pt on 13pt Mrs Eaves Serif Narrow
Printed and bound in England

# Foreword

## by Samuel D. Gruber
### President, International Survey of Jewish Monuments

Who would expect a book about the synagogues of Central and Western Pennsylvania to be an adventure story—a book about hopes, dreams, hard work and heartache? And yet, through a collection of over 200 photographs, that is what Julian H. Preisler provides. He takes us on a journey through a largely unknown and mostly forgotten history of Jewish settlement, community building and, too often, community dispersion, in a few big cities, but mostly small and mid-size towns in Pennsylvania, where Jews have settled and prospered often from the glare and blare of national media, and sometimes hidden in plain sight from national Jewish institutions and organizations.

With the exception of Pittsburgh (and Philadelphia in the East) Pennsylvania Jews have been mostly small town Jews, hard-working Main Street Jews, family-oriented middle class Jews, and patriotic American Jews. First as peddlers, then as shop owners, and occasionally as chain store or department store magnates; and later as teachers, accountants, doctors, lawyers, and engineers, they followed the opening of farm country, oil fields, coal mines, steel mills, and all the growing industry of Central and Western Pennsylvania. Almost everywhere they settled—a few families here, a few more there—they founded a Jewish cemetery, a Benevolent Society, perhaps a B'nai B'rith Lodge, and they built a synagogue—and sometimes more than one. It is in these synagogue buildings (past and present) that one sees that sense of belonging to something bigger, to a world of Judaism and Jewish tradition. In the location, size and architecture of the synagogues, one also sees the frequent clash of aspirations and practical considerations. Sometimes a tiny community could scrape up enough money to build something simple and useful. Occasionally, a small community tried to make something grand (as in the 1897 synagogue of Oil City). Styles reflected national trends tempered by local taste and context. The Jewish "church" needed to be distinct—but to fit in, too.

These photos take us on an architectural journey, as well. Almost every style of American synagogue architecture can be found in some form in towns and cities of Pennsylvania. The 1890s, 1920s, and 1950–60s were all periods of rapid change. Creative variations of Gothic, Romanesque, Moorish, Classical, Byzantine, Deco, and Modern examples abound. Simply, they reflect the diversity of Jewish taste, but through more careful analysis of architectural forms, decorative symbols and even the language of inscriptions something about the congregations that built them. We can understand broad changes in style and taste, but also internal congregational change when we see what kind of building a congregation left behind, and what sort of new structure they chose to build. Were they originally from Central or Eastern Europe? Were they first generation or third generation Americans? Were these Reform or Orthodox Jews? Did they look east to Philadelphia and New York or west to Pittsburgh and Cincinnati for inspiration? Were they assimilationist, or maybe Zionist? Did they see themselves of part of a larger American community, or were they creating a new American version of the old closed "shtetl"? Were these Pennsylvania Jews backward or forward looking in outlook; traditional or modern?

Julian Preisler has provided us a great service with this book, and a great deal to consider. These images and the history he provides are only the beginning. Until now, we have known more about communities and synagogue architecture in places like central Slovakia or western Ukraine than central and western Pennsylvania. What Preisler has found is a gift—a new look at what it meant (and means) to be an American Jew. New York and Los Angeles may be poles of American Jewish identity, but there are so many interesting people and places in between. Preisler helps us fill in the empty spaces, and provides a whole new collection of buildings to help write an expanded history of American Jewish architecture.

# Preface

Why is a book like this important? This is a question many people ask me as I do research on America's synagogues, current and former. I have been interested in history and architecture since I was very young, and synagogue architecture specifically since I was an early teenager in Columbus, Ohio. Buildings fascinate me, and I am drawn to synagogues. This is my passion and it is vital that we document the "built" Jewish environment and share what is learned. One of my hobbies is to photograph synagogues, especially former ones. To me there is a great feeling of discovery to find out about a former synagogue that has been forgotten by time and do my part to bring that history to the present. Synagogues, cemeteries, Jewish Community Centers and other such buildings associated with a Jewish community stand as a testament to our history, and future. Placing importance on our past must be made as important as the time and energy we give to the present and future of our communities. This book takes as its purpose the identification and documentation of the synagogues of Central & Western Pennsylvania, whether they are current or former congregations. It is a visual recording of these buildings and, as such, represents what physically exists today.

The former synagogues featured in the book are an especially important part of this process because they can easily be forgotten. In so many of these locations the well-known Jewish stores, businesses and names that were a fixture of daily life in a community are long gone, but an old synagogue stands as a physical reminder that, yes, there once was a vital Jewish community here. During the process of my research, I made the decision to include a few images of demolished synagogues. For some former Jewish Communities in Central and Western Pennsylvania, the only physical vestige of the Jewish community is the cemetery and I wanted to give an additional visual look at what once existed. With that in mind this is not a catalog nor complete history of all synagogues and congregations that have existed in the area, but it is a huge record nonetheless and is probably one of the most complete. Every effort was made to ensure the accuracy of the information contained in the book. In some instances very little information was available, or what was available was vague or inconsistent. As to the organization of the book, I did take a few minor liberties deciding what locations would be included in either Central or Western Pennsylvania. I ask the reader's indulgence. I provided English translations of the Hebrew names of the congregations in the book. I did not give a translation in each instance or for similar versions of some names. It was interesting to learn all the varied spellings. As my research is always on-going I welcome the reader's input and any potential corrections. Enjoy these wonderful images as I have and continue to do so. May this book inspire additional research and documentation.

# Dedication

This book is dedicated to the generations that have come before us and to the future generations that will continue Jewish life in so many of the communities featured in the book. It is also dedicated to those people who are ensuring that the history of those Jewish communities that no longer have an active Jewish presence is recorded and preserved so that this history will not be lost. The support and encouragement of family is and always has been an important part of my work. I thank my family and loved ones for their patience and for always encouraging me to do the work that I love.

# Acknowledgments

An undertaking such as this cannot be completed without hundreds of hours of research, photography, planning, and the interest and enthusiasm of Jewish congregations, historical societies, and archives throughout the region covered. Thankfully there were only a few congregations that, for some reason, were not interested in my research and did not respond to my communications. I could not have completed this extensive book without the help of the many synagogues that graciously provided photographs, historical data, and, in many cases, some very unique historical images. I would like to extend a special thank you to several people and institutions that were especially helpful and cooperative in bringing this research to fruition. My thanks go to Susan Melnick, Archivist at the Rauh Jewish Archives at the Senator John Heinz History Center in Pittsburgh, for all her efforts to help me with information and historic images for the book. I am grateful that the Rauh Jewish Archive waived all copying and publication fees for me, which was a very generous gesture. I also would like to extend a special thank you to Barry Rudel, the Johnstown Jewish community and the Johnstown Area Historical Association for their assistance with present-day and historical images, and also for waiving their publication fees. Their recognition of the importance of historical research and the process of sharing history with the general public is much appreciated. Thanks must go to so many wonderful people and congregations that were helpful to me, expressed interest in the book and the importance of the research, and gave me a lot of encouragement. A huge thank you goes to Richard W. Clark for all his editing and proof-reading.

I extend a sincere and heartfelt thank you to the following persons and synagogues. This book could not have been completed without your help. I hope that I have remembered everyone in the following list: Scott Allen (Beth Shalom, Pittsburgh); Ira Beckerman (Beth Shalom, Mechanicsburg); Jack Bergstein (Beth Am, Monessen); Temple Beth Israel (Altoona); Beth Shalom Congregation (Pittsburgh); Congregation B'nai Abraham (Butler); Karen Bowman (North Cambria); Lee Chottiner (Pittsburgh Jewish Chronicle); Julie Cohen (Temple David, Monroeville); Arnold W. Cushner; Richard D'Loss (Ahavath Achim, Carnegie); Naomi Drezner (Beth Yehuda, Lock Haven); Cindy Elder (Montour County Genealogical Society); Emanue-El Israel Congregation (Greensburgh); Dan Grabenstein (Kesher Israel, Harrisburg); Hannah Maia Frishberg (Indiana); Todd Halpern (Rockville, Maryland); Hans Jonas (Jonas Photography, Pittsburgh); Martin Kanovsky; Larry Kapenstein (B'nai Jacob, Middletown); Jack E. Kapp (Philadelphia); Hank Katzen (Orlando, Florida); Rabbi Peter Kessler (Ohev Sholom, Harrisburg); Robbie Kurland; Larry Lawson (Beth El, Bradford); Dick Leffel (B'nai Israel, White Oak); Jackie Leicht (Ohev Shalom, Pittsburgh); Joel B. Lench, MD; Gail Levine (Parkway Jewish

9

Center, Pittsburgh); Linda Levine (Pittsburgh); Richard Steven Levine; Ted Matlow; Michael S. Melnick (Pittsburgh); Tony Miga (Pittsburgh); Holly Mollo (Agudath Achim, Huntingdon); Gail Murray (Beth Samuel, Ambridge); Richard Myerowitz (Temple David, Monroeville); Dr. Bernard D. Newman (Adat Shalom, Pittsburgh); Jane Ellen Nickell (Meadville); Rabbi David Ostrich, Brit Shalom, State College); Bruce Pratt (Titusville); Linda Raden (Temple Sinai, Pittsburgh); Saralouise Reis (Temple Emanuel, Pittsburgh); Clifford Rieders (Ohev Sholom, Williamsport); Rodef Shalom Congregation (Martha Berg, Lauren Wolcott—Pittsburgh); Jill Rook (Adat Shalom, Pittsburgh); Howard L. Ross; Barry Rudel, (Beth Sholom, Johnstown); Robin Schuldenfrei (Harrisburg); Mary Scutella (Anshe Hesed, Erie); Carol Shapiro (Ohev Sholom, York); Jim Stein; Linda Stewart; Susan Sussman (Chisuk Emuna, Harrisburg); Marian Ungar Davis (Pittsburgh); Rachel Weinblum (Beth Israel, Pittsburgh); Eleanor Zimmerman, zl' (Beth Yehuda, Lock Haven).

# Introduction

With the second largest Jewish population in the world, the United States has thousands of synagogues; they come in all shapes and sizes, ranging from small, simple structures, to historic and ornate facilities. Synagogues can be found in small towns, cities, and suburban communities, and sometimes in out-of-the-way places. Pennsylvania is unique with regard to the number of locations that either have, or once had, functioning Jewish congregations. They can be found, of course, in large numbers in Pittsburgh and Philadelphia, but they are also found in the smaller cities, as well as a multitude of small towns across the state. Some of these locations were once industrial and manufacturing giants and had more than one Jewish congregation. The diversity of synagogues and locations in Pennsylvania is, in my opinion, unique in the United States. By gathering and presenting images of these many synagogues, especially the ones that are no longer used for Jewish worship, not only is their history documented, but the uniqueness and wealth of architecture is shared for all. The diversity of Jewish architecture in Pennsylvania reflects the rich diversity of the Jewish communities that settled in the Commonwealth.

Jewish life thrives, not surprisingly, in Pittsburgh and Harrisburg, but it also is strong in some of the smaller cities of central and western Pennsylvania such as Altoona, Erie, Johnstown, Williamsport and York. Many smaller cities, such as Johnstown and Uniontown, once had substantial Jewish Communities and several synagogues, but today are no longer manufacturing and industrial hubs. As a result, the Jewish population has declined in numbers. Many of these locations still have small, but dedicated Jewish congregations that continue the tradition of Jewish worship, philanthropy, education and community. Sadly, there are too many towns or boroughs that no longer have Jewish populations or functioning synagogues. Many of these buildings still stand and are used for other purposes, some more appropriate than others. Many buildings have been demolished, but thankfully, in most cases, some photographic records exist to document these structures. Change is natural part of the life of a community; documenting and recording the past for future generations ensures that the change we experience does not negate what came before.

# Central Pennsylvania

**Altoona**, located in Blair County, in the Allegheny Mountains, has long been known as a railroad hub, having been established in 1849 by the Pennsylvania Railroad. Railroads, and the industries associated with them, thrived in the region, while Altoona became an economic and cultural center. Much like other Rust-Belt cities, Altoona suffered decline as industry changed and relocated, and the railroads no longer held their former prominence. Today, Altoona is known as the "Mountain City" and has expanded its tourist sector with regard to railroad history and the city's scenic location. Altoona is home to Sheetz, the popular convenience store chain, the Penn State Altoona campus, and it has a downtown that has seen much restoration and revitalization.

Jews have been a part of the region since the nineteenth century. The organized Jewish community dates to 1874, when the first congregation was established as the Mountain City Reformed Congregation. This eventually became Temple Beth Israel. The second synagogue, Agudath Achim, was established originally as an Orthodox congregation in 1883. Despite being a smaller Jewish community, Altoona boasts a Jewish Federation and a variety of Jewish groups. The Jewish Memorial Center, opened in 1949, now serves as a sports center for the community at large; it still holds some Jewish activities and serves as the home of the local Jewish Federation. The synagogues in town are beautiful historic structures that are well-cared for by their active and dedicated congregations. The large Mount Sinai Jewish Cemetery outside the city has sections for both Beth Israel and for Agudath Achim.

**Harrisburg,** in Dauphin County, is the state capital and the hub of political life in Pennsylvania. It is also the largest Jewish community in the Central Pennsylvania region. Jewish Communities located in state capitals are not always the largest in a state, but they hold a special prominence, given their geopolitical location. Jews, originally from Germany and England, settled in Harrisburg in the 1840s and were the first Jews to settle in the city. The first Jewish congregation formed in Harrisburg was Temple Ohev Sholom. Twenty-four Jewish families gathered for worship during the High Holy Days in 1853. Two years later, the Orthodox congregation acquired land for a cemetery and, in 1865, the first synagogue in the capital city was dedicated at Second and South Streets. The congregation became Reform in 1867. The second congregation established was the Orthodox Chisuk Emuna in 1883. The Orthodox Kesher Israel was established in 1902 followed by the Orthodox Machzikey Hadas Congregation (later Chabad-Lubavitch) in 1904. The Beth El Temple was formed in 1926 as the first Conservative congregation in the city. The early Jewish community was centered on the downtown area in the vicinity of the state capitol building.

As the Jewish population moved uptown, many of the old synagogues were sold, and the area used for the expansion of the capitol complex. Ohev Sholom and Beth El's present historic synagogues are situated uptown on Front Street along the Susquehanna River. Congregations were also established in Middletown (B'nai Jacob f. 1904) and Steelton (Tifereth Israel f. 1904) and in the Cumberland County boroughs of Carlisle (Beth Tikvah f. 1972) and Mechanicsburg (Beth Shalom f. 1970). From the early years to the 1940s, most Harrisburg Jews were engaged in the retail trades, particularly food, clothing and furniture. By the 1960s, local Jews were also engaged in manufacturing and food distribution, as well as the professions and state government, in which most in the Jewish community work today. Harrisburg has a very active and large Jewish Community Center and all manner of Jewish groups, organizations, and schools exist within the Greater Harrisburg Jewish community. There are several Jewish cemeteries in the area serving the Harrisburg, Carlisle, and Mechanicsburg Jewish communities. A Holocaust memorial was dedicated in 1977 at the Jewish Community Center. In Riverfront Park, along the Susquehanna River, stands the Holocaust Memorial for the Commonwealth of Pennsylvania. Designed by noted artist, David Ascalon, the memorial was dedicated in 1994 and recently was restored. The cemetery for Beth El Temple also has a Holocaust memorial dedicated in 1998.

**Williamsport,** in Lycoming County, known nationwide as the home of Little League Baseball, is also home to a small but thriving Jewish community with two synagogues and a long history. The first recorded Jewish person in the area of Williamsport was Solomon Huffman, a peddler who was killed in 1838 with robbery as the motive. By the 1840s there were several German Jewish families who had settled in Williamsport and opened various businesses in town. Informal religious services were held, and as more Jewish families came to the area, talk began about establishing a formal congregation. The influx of Jews to the area was temporarily interrupted by the Civil War. In 1863, a Jewish cemetery was dedicated and, in 1866, the first Jewish congregation in Williamsport, Temple Beth Ha-Shalom, was formally chartered. They laid the cornerstone of the first synagogue in town in 1871. The building served as the home of the congregation until 1901, when severe flooding that year exacerbated damage from a prior flood in 1889, and weakened the building to the extent that it had to be vacated. A new synagogue was dedicated in 1904 and still serves as the home of Beth Ha-Shalom. As more Jews of Eastern European origin settled in Williamsport, another more traditional congregation was established to meet the needs of these new members of the Jewish community who preferred the Orthodox form of worship. Ohev Sholom congregation was incorporated in 1905 as Orthodox, but had existed as a congregation for some years prior. The congregation joined the Conservative movement in the 1950s but is now an unaffiliated Traditional congregation. Their present synagogue was built in 1951. Beginning in 1991, about a dozen stained glass windows were designed and installed at the synagogue. The work was done by local artist Peter Koch. Williamsport has two Jewish cemeteries to serve the community. A Holocaust Memorial can be found at the Ohev Sholom Cemetery.

**York** is an historic Pennsylvania city founded in 1741 by settlers from Philadelphia. York is rich in Colonial and revolutionary era history, as well as Civil War history. It was the largest northern city to be occupied by Confederate forces. In the years following the Civil War, the city became an important manufacturing center. Elijah and Shinah Etting are thought to be the first

Jewish settlers in York having arrived from Lancaster around 1758. They set up a small store and became well-known for their hospitality and generosity. In 1780, just two years after the death of her husband, Shina Etting moved with her eight children to Baltimore, Maryland. It was not until 1847 when another Jewish family, the Lehymeyers, came to York and opened a store.

The present, organized, Jewish community traces its beginnings to 1877 when twenty-four Jewish families came together to form the Hebrew Reformed Congregation, now known as Temple Beth Israel. A Jewish burial ground on South George Street was established a few years earlier with the first burial taking place in 1871. That small cemetery downtown was recently cleaned and restored. Later in the nineteenth century, Jews of Eastern European origin settled in York and set up their own Orthodox congregations. Anshe Hadas was organized in 1883. Adas Israel Congregation was established in 1900, and their 1904 synagogue was located at Pershing Avenue near College Avenue. In 1902, the members of Anshe Hadas resolved to build a synagogue and decided to change their name to Ohev Sholom. Their synagogue was dedicated in 1904 at Pershing Avenue and Princess Street. Both buildings of Adas Israel and Ohev Sholom were demolished in the late 1960s for the expansion of the William Penn Senior High School. Ohev Sholom Congregation adopted the Conservative form of worship in 1953. When Ohev Sholom built their new synagogue on Eastern Boulevard in 1967 or 1968, the remaining membership of the Adas Israel Congregation merged with them. It was not until 1907 that Beth Israel Congregation built their first synagogue at 129 South Beaver Street. It was built with a mix of Moorish and Byzantine elements. As the congregation grew in size, larger facilities were needed. A new synagogue and sanctuary were completed in 1962 and 1966 on Hollywood Drive, where the congregation is located today. The old synagogue on South Beaver is now a Catholic church. Ohev Sholom now shares space with Beth Israel as their Eastern Boulevard synagogue was sold in 2006 and subsequently razed. York has a large Jewish Community Center which began downtown in 1910. Since 1989, they have been located adjacent to Temple Beth Israel. A large Holocaust Memorial wall sculpture was dedicated in the Jewish Community Center lobby in 1997. There are several Jewish cemeteries in the York area serving the community.

Mention should also be made of the small Jewish community that still exists in Hanover, also in York County. Jews of Bavarian origin settled in Hanover around 1826 and organized a synagogue and cemetery. The small Jewish community had thirteen families, but existed only until about 1870. Unfortunately, their small cemetery outside of town was vandalized and neglected once the Jewish community ceased to exist, and what remained was flooded in the 1930s in order to make way for a man-made lake. A small village and several farms were also flooded to create the lake. The Hanover Jewish community was revived in the mid-twentieth century, and incorporated as the Hanover Hebrew Congregation 1941. In 1949, a small house was purchased and converted for use as a synagogue. It still serves as the home today of the small Conservative congregation, one of the smallest in the United States.

Altoona, Blair County—Congregation Agudath Achim was established in 1883 and chartered on March 17, 1885 as an Orthodox congregation. Their first synagogue was a simple yet beautiful frame structure. It was built in 1895 and located at 1306 17$^{th}$ Street. In 1934 the congregation moved away from Orthodoxy and adopted the Conservative form of worship and ritual. *Sketch courtesy of Agudath Achim Congregation, Altoona, n.d.*

Altoona, Blair County—The present synagogue of Agudath Achim Congregation was dedicated in 1924 and located on the same site as the original 1895 synagogue structure. A new modern wing was added on to the synagogue in 1971. The front of the new wing contains a large sculpture of the "Burning Bush." *Sketch courtesy of Agudath Achim Congregation, n.d.*

Altoona, Blair County—The buff brick façade of the present Agudath Achim synagogue features intricate designs in stone of the Star of David along with grapes, vines and leaves. *Photograph by Stanford Lembeck and courtesy of the Center for the Study of Jewish Life in Central Pennsylvania, 2011*

Altoona, Blair County—Temple Beth Israel began during the latter half of the nineteenth century. The first known record of the congregation dates to 1874. The Mount Sinai Jewish Cemetery has been in use since 1873. In 1877 the congregation adopted the Reform liturgy and practice, and was renamed Mountain City Hebrew Reformed Congregation. Their first synagogue was built in 1896 at 13th Avenue and 15th Street. It featured a beige stone exterior, onion dome towers and Moorish style arches. It is presently used as a church. *Photograph by Mark Gordon, 2005*

Altoona, Blair County—In 1922, Mountain City Hebrew Reformed Congregation became Temple Beth Israel. The present synagogue was built in 1924 at 3004 Union Avenue in the Mansion Park neighborhood. The beige brick synagogue features a large, tiled dome over the sanctuary and numerous beautiful stained glass windows. *Photograph by June Weston, 2007*

Berwick, Columbia County—By 1903 there were two Jewish congregations in Berwick—one Sephardic and one Ahskenazic. By the time Ohev Sholom's synagogue was destroyed by fire in 1953, it was the only synagogue in town. It was rebuilt and again damaged by fire in 1986. Rebuilt once again, the synagogue closed in 1997 due to a lack of Jews living in the area. Ohev Sholom was originally Orthodox but later became Conservative. The former synagogue became the Berwick Health Wellness Foundation in 1998 and is currently the local headquarters of the Red Cross. The Jewish cemetery is cared for by Temple Israel in Wilkes-Barre. *Photograph by Kerry Jean Norce, 1991*

Bloomsburg, Columbia County—Congregation Beth Israel was established in 1926 and is located in downtown Bloomsburg at 144 West Fourth Street. The red brick synagogue, which was originally built as a church, features beautiful Jewish-themed stained glass windows installed by Beth Israel and was purchased in 1926. Beth Israel has been an unaffiliated Reform congregation since its founding in 1926 and holds services and dinners on most holidays and festivals. *Photograph by Dani Crossley, 2007*

Chambersburg, Franklin County—The roots of a Jewish community in Franklin County date back to 1840 when local Jews of German origin established a Jewish burial society and consecrated a cemetery in 1844. This was the first Jewish cemetery to be established outside of Philadelphia. The original Jewish community declined by 1900. In 1919, a group of new Jewish residents banned together and the Sons of Israel Congregation was chartered. In 1939 a former church downtown at King and Second Streets was purchased and remodeled for use as a synagogue and is still used today. *Photograph by Julian H. Preisler, 2011*

Chambersburg, Franklin County—
The synagogue has simple exterior
decorations on the doors and windows
above. In 1940, a Mennonite resident of
Chambersburg designed and created
the Ark and wood carvings that decorate
the Bimah and wall behind the Bimah.
It was his gift to the congregation
and a "token of his affection for the
Children of Israel." The Sons of Israel
Congregation is a small but active
community. *Photograph by Julian H.
Preisler, 2011*

Danville, Montour County—Jews of
German origin settled in Danville
prior to when Congregation B'nai Zion
was chartered in 1854. Their original
synagogue built in 1853 was replaced by a
newer, ornate synagogue. It was built in
1871 at a time when the streets of Danville
were still unpaved. Jews of Russian origin
settled in Danville beginning about
1881. Because of cultural and language
differences, two Jewish cemeteries were
established. Around 1915, the two groups
united. The congregation lasted until the
mid-twentieth century. Unfortunately,
much of the history and records of the
congregation were lost due to flooding
from Hurricane Agnes in 1972. Vintage
image courtesy of Cindy Elder of the
Montour County Genealogical Society.
Originally published in *Remembering The
Past: A Photo History of the Danville Area* by
the former Danville News, n.d.

Harrisburg, Dauphin County—Beth El Temple was formed in 1926 and was the first Conservative congregation to be established in Harrisburg. Their Byzantine-Revival style synagogue was built in 1928 at 2637 North Front Street in the Uptown area of Harrisburg. The congregation, today, is the largest Jewish congregation in the area. *Photograph by Julian H. Preisler, 2013*

Harrisburg, Dauphin County—The entrance to Beth El Temple faces the beautiful Susquehanna River. The synagogue with its unique architectural style and Star of David on top of the sanctuary roof is a well-known landmark in the city. *Photograph by Julian H. Preisler, 2013*

Harrisburg, Dauphin County—The interior of the Beth El Temple sanctuary was completely remodeled and also had new stained glass windows installed since this 2007 interior photograph was taken. *Photograph by Arthur Rosenthol, 2007*

Harrisburg, Dauphin County—Chisuk Emuna Congregation was established as an Orthodox congregation in 1883 by Jewish immigrants from Lithuania. There would be three buildings before the North Division Street synagogue was built in 1956. By then the congregation had become Conservative. The brown and beige brick synagogue featured two small round windows each with a Star of David on each side of the entrance, plus clerestory windows in the sanctuary. The synagogue was severely damaged by a fire in 2009 and services moved to the Jewish Community Center. *Vintage image courtesy of Chisuk Emuna Congregation*

Harrisburg, Dauphin County—The Mid-Century Modern style sanctuary of the North Division Street synagogue of Chisuk Emuna Congregation featured a stone Ark surround and grill-work at the front of the sanctuary with Judaic symbols. *Vintage image courtesy of Chisuk Emuna Congregation, c. 1957*

Harrisburg, Dauphin County—Chisuk Emuna decided to build a new contemporary synagogue as a result of the 2009 fire. In 2013, they dedicated a new four million dollar synagogue and school located at 3219 Green Street just north of the old synagogue. The old fire-ravaged synagogue on Division Street was sold and is now home to a reform-minded Islamic mosque. *Photography by Robin Schuldenfrei and courtesy of CAVU Creative, 2013*

Harrisburg, Dauphin County—Kesher Israel is the only Orthodox congregation in Harrisburg and was organized in 1902. Their former synagogue was built in 1918 at Capitol and Briggs Street. That synagogue was sold when the current synagogue uptown was built. The Capitol Street synagogue was demolished to facilitate the expansion of the capital complex downtown. *Vintage Image Courtesy of Kesher Israel Congregation, n.d.*

Harrisburg, Dauphin County—A new Mid-Century Modern synagogue for Kesher Israel was built at 2500 North Third Street in 1949. An adjacent educational wing was completed in 1963. The congregation is smaller today than it was in 1949 and the present facility is now for sale. Plans are being made to find a smaller, more suitable space for the congregation. *Photograph by Julian H. Preisler, 2013*

Harrisburg, Dauphin County—The beautiful sanctuary of Kesher Israel contains the ornate Ark and pews from the previous synagogue building on Capitol Street. The wall behind the Ark is white marble. There is a large Star of David shaped light fixture in the sanctuary ceiling. *Photograph by Daniel Grabenstein and courtesy of Kesher Israel, 2013*

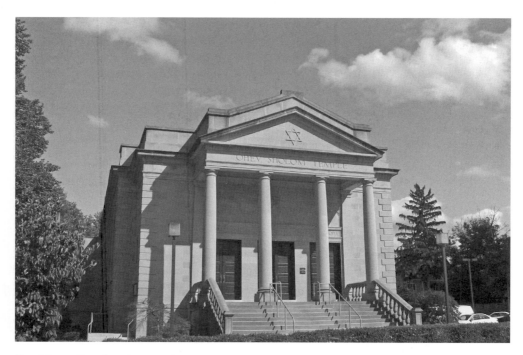

Harrisburg, Dauphin County—Ohev Sholom Congregation was established in 1853 as an Orthodox congregation by 24 Jewish families. It was the first Jewish congregation to be formed in Harrisburg. The first Jewish cemetery was established by the congregation in 1855. Today, Ohev Sholom is located in a Classical-Revival style synagogue that was dedicated in 1920 at 2345 North Front Street. *Photograph by Julian H. Preisler, 2013*

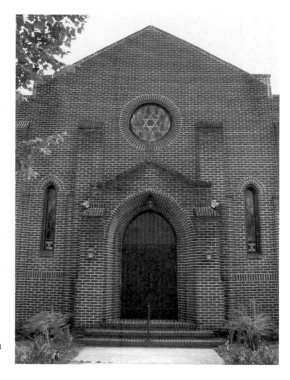

Huntingdon, Huntingdon County—Agudath Achim Congregation was incorporated in 1920. In 1930, their red brick synagogue at 1009 Washington Street was dedicated. The congregation experienced substantial decline by the 1970s to 1980s, but in recent years has experienced somewhat of a rebirth. In 2010, through a partnership with the local Hillel chapter, the congregation dedicated its synagogue facilities as the Faith Isaacson Juniata College Hillel House. The Agudath Achim Memorial Park serves as the local Jewish cemetery. *Photograph by Julian H. Preisler, 2013*

Huntingdon, Huntingdon County—Agudath Achim's elegant synagogue features Romanesque style details and beautiful stained glass windows including a Star of David window above the entrance. The synagogue is well maintained and located in a residential area near the center of town. The congregation is Independent/Reform in ritual and practice. *Photograph by Julian H. Preisler, 2013*

Lewistown, Mifflin County—The Ohev Sholom Congregation was an Orthodox congregation chartered in 1912. Organized religious services began in 1908; there had been Jewish settlers in town as early as 1862. The synagogue, located at 20 East 3$^{rd}$ Street, was dedicated in 1920 and expanded in 1929. A large Community Center addition was dedicated in 1952 and a Jewish cemetery was dedicated in 1940. The synagogue proper is shown after the synagogue was sold, but prior to being repainted. *Photograph by Stanford Lembeck and courtesy of the Center for the Study of Jewish Life in Central Pennsylvania, 2011*

Lewistown, Mifflin County—The Lumina Center, a local Methodist youth outreach center, purchased the former Jewish Community Center building of Ohev Sholom in 1995 and purchased the synagogue proper in 2010. The local Jewish community unfortunately no longer had enough members for a functioning synagogue. The former synagogue and community center were repainted in vivid colors for use as the youth center. The Hebrew cornerstones for both buildings and stained glass windows on the side of the synagogue remain. *Photograph by Julian H. Preisler, 2013*

Lewistown, Mifflin County—Ohev Sholom's sanctuary interior looking towards the Ark, just prior to the closing and sale of the synagogue. *Photograph by Mark Widome, 2010, and courtesy of Iris B. Sitkin*

Lock Haven, Clinton County—German Jews came to Lock Haven as early as 1840 from nearby Pottsville. By 1880, Eastern European Jews began settling in the area as well. Congregation Beth Yehudah was chartered in 1904, but had been in existence for some years prior to 1900. Their first synagogue was built in 1904 at West Clinton and Commerce Streets. It still stands, but has been remodeled for residential use. The present synagogue at 320 West Church Street was dedicated in 1952. Originally Orthodox, the small congregation has recently been affiliated with the Reform movement. Their cemetery dates to the 1880s and contains the section once known as the German Jewish Cemetery. *Photograph by Julian H. Preisler, 2013*

Lock Haven, Clinton County—Beth Yehuda's synagogue contains many colorful, modern-style stained glass windows, as well as Ark doors. The synagogue building was recently given to a consortium associated with the Lock Haven University. The congregation has use of the synagogue without the financial drain on the small congregation. They also have the knowledge that the building's legacy will remain even when the congregation someday is no more. *Photograph by Richard W. Clark, 2013*

Mechanicsburg, Cumberland County—Temple Beth Shalom (House of Peace) was the first Jewish congregation established outside of Harrisburg proper. It was formed in 1970, and their synagogue at 913 Allendale Road was dedicated in 1974. The synagogue is located in a residential area and was extensively renovated in 2003. In 1982 the congregation affiliated with the Reconstructionist movement and is the only Reconstructionist synagogue in Central Pennsylvania. *Photograph by Ira Beckerman and courtesy of Temple Beth Shalom, 2013*

Mechanicsburg, Cumberland County—The sanctuary of Temple Beth Shalom, under construction. The land for the synagogue was donated by a member family, Kranzel, and the construction was done largely by congregation members. *Photograph courtesy of Temple Beth Shalom, 1974*

Mechanicsburg, Cumberland County—The original design by Victor J. Sigiana for Temple Beth Shalom was a bit more elaborate than what was eventually built. This is often the case, and most congregations faced with the enormous financial responsibility of building a house of worship must scale down their ideas and wishes with regard to building size and design. *Architectural Sketch courtesy of Temple Beth Shalom, n.d.*

Middletown, Dauphin County—By the early 1900s there were about twenty Jewish families residing in Middletown outside of Harrisburg. They came together in 1904 to form B'nai Jacob as an Orthodox congregation. The neo-Gothic red brick synagogue at Nissley and Water Streets was built in 1906 and is listed on the National Register of Historic Places. The synagogue was designed and built by the charter members of the congregation and is now the oldest synagogue in continuous use in Dauphin County. Today B'nai Jacob is an unaffiliated Egalitarian/Conservative congregation. *Photograph by Jack E. Kapp, Kapptured Moments Photography, Philadelphia, 2010*

Mount Carmel, Northumberland County—Jewish religious services were first held here in 1887, and the Orthodox Tifereth Israel Congregation was incorporated in 1896. Their synagogue was built in 1922 at 135 South Maple Street and contained many beautiful stained glass windows. As local industry disappeared and the Jewish population declined, the synagogue was closed and sold in 1986 to the Masons. In 1988, the building was dedicated as the new Masonic Hall Cedar Lodge. There is also a Jewish cemetery in Mount Carmel. *Photograph courtesy of Ted Matlow and Howard L. Ross*

Philipsburg, Centre County—The Sons of Israel Congregation is a former synagogue located at 6th and Spruce Streets. The congregation was most likely originally Orthodox and established in the early twentieth century. The Hebrew Cemetery in South Philipsburg has graves dating as early as 1900. The Philipsburg Hebrew Association appears to be the caretaker of the cemetery today. The synagogue closed in the 1990s, and artifacts including the Torah scrolls were given to Congregation Brit Shalom in nearby State College. Phillipsburg is located in both Centre and Clearfield Counties. *Photograph by J. Nolan, 2007*

Shamokin, Northumberland County—B'nai Israel is a former synagogue located at 7 East Sunbury Street. The Orthodox congregation was established in 1903, and the synagogue was built in 1921. B'nai Israel closed sometime between 1998 and 2007 and sold their building due to a decline in the local Jewish population. The former synagogue now serves as a community mission and church. Much of the exterior ornamentation and stained glass windows remain. There is also a Jewish cemetery in use since 1895, located in adjacent Coal Township. *Photograph by Julian H. Preisler, 2013*

Shamokin, Northumberland County—A close-up of the façade of the former B'nai Israel shows the ornate details and stained glass windows of the beige brick and stone synagogue. It was a rather ornate building for what was a smaller size Jewish community, and this might have been an indication of the success of many of the members of the former Jewish community. *Photograph by Julian H. Preisler, 2013*

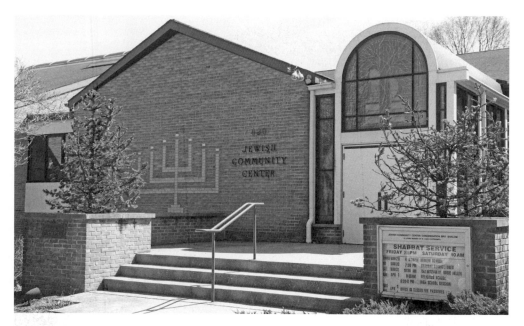

State College, Centre County—Brit Shalom is a Reform congregation which traces its roots to the Jewish Community Council of Bellefonte and State College formed in 1954 and incorporated in 1956. Prior to that, beginning in the 1930s, Jewish families from Bellefonte and State College worshiped at Hillel at Penn State University. The Hillel building was used for activities until 1965, when the original portion of what became the synagogue was dedicated at 620 East Hamilton Avenue. In 1983 a purpose-built Sanctuary was added. There is a Jewish section of a local cemetery in town and also a small Jewish cemetery in the nearby town of Bellefonte. *Photograph courtesy of Congregation Brit Shalom, n.d.*

State College, Centre County—Shown here is a slightly different view of the original Jewish Community Center portion of the synagogue. In 1979 the name Congregation Brit Shalom was added. Brit Shalom was associated with Reconstructionist Judaism from 1987 to 2001 when it officially joined the Reform movement. Brith Shalom has, in recent years, become the repository of artifacts and items from synagogues that have closed in the region. *Photograph by Stanford Lembeck and courtesy of the Center for the Study of Jewish Life in Central Pennsylvania, 2011*

State College,
Centre County—
The Ark and
Eternal Light in
the sanctuary at
Congregation
Brit Shalom are
both simple and
dramatic in design.
*Photograph courtesy
of Congregation Brit
Shalom, n.d.*

Steelton, Dauphin County—Tifereth Israel Synagogue was an Orthodox congregation organized in 1904 in Steelton outside of Harrisburg. Their synagogue was built in 1906 at 9 North 2$^{nd}$ Street. The congregation closed in the 1970s, and the synagogue was demolished shortly thereafter. The cornerstone from the synagogue was saved and is now on the grounds of the B'nai Jacob synagogue in Middletown. *Photograph by Jack E. Kapp, Kapptured Moments Photography, Philadelphia, 2013*

Sunbury, Northumberland County—Congregation Beth El is a Liberal-Unaffiliated congregation located at 249 Arch Street. The congregation was chartered in 1911, and beginning in 1919 a former church was used as the synagogue. A new synagogue was completed on the same site in 2007 after a 3 year project. It is the only synagogue in the five-county region today with a full-time rabbi. There is also a Jewish cemetery in Sunbury. *Photograph by Julian H. Preisler, 2013*

Sunbury, Northumberland County—The synagogue was designed by the noted firm of Venturi, Scott Brown & Associates, Inc. of Philadelphia. It has a sanctuary, social hall, library, classrooms, interior courtyard and kosher dairy kitchen. The sanctuary has an angled ceiling surrounded by clear windows that let in natural light. *Photograph by Julian H. Preisler, 2013*

Williamsport, Lycoming County—Temple Beth Ha-Shalom is a Reform congregation located at 425 Center Street. In 1866, the congregation was formally chartered, and the first synagogue in town was built in 1871. That building served as the home of the congregation until 1901 when severe flooding over the years weakened the building to the extent that it had to be vacated. A new synagogue was dedicated in 1904 and still serves as the home of Beth Ha-Shalom. A school and social hall were added in 1923 and 1961. *Photograph by Julian H. Preisler, 2013*

Williamsport, Lycoming County—Temple Beth Ha-Shalom contains impressive stained glass windows from 1904 that were completely restored between 2010 and 2012. The large and impressive synagogue continues to serve the small Reform Jewish community today in Williamsport. It is one of the oldest Jewish congregations in North Central Pennsylvania. *Photograph by Julian H. Preisler, 2013*

Williamsport, Lycoming County—As Jews of Eastern European origin settled in Williamsport, need arose for a congregation that met their desire for the Orthodox form of worship. Ohev Sholom Congregation was incorporated in 1905 but existed as a congregation for some year prior. Their first synagogue was dedicated in 1915 on Edwin Street. That building no longer exists. In 1951 the present synagogue center at 1501 Cherry Street was dedicated. *Photograph by Julian H. Preisler, 2013*

Williamsport, Lycoming County—Congregation Ohev Sholom joined the Conservative movement in the 1950s and later moved back towards the Orthodox form of worship. It is now an unaffiliated Traditional congregation. A dozen modern stained glass windows of varying topics were added to the synagogue beginning in 1991. They were designed by local artist Peter Koch. *Photograph by Steven Bonnell, 2007*

York, York County—Beth Israel Congregation, the first in York, was established in 1877 as the Hebrew Reformed Congregation Temple Beth Israel. Their first synagogue was built in 1907 at South Beaver Street and Newton Alley. That same year the congregation voted to join the Reform movement. As the local Jewish population moved away from the center of town, Beth Israel relocated to their new facility on Hollywood Drive in 1962. Their large sanctuary was dedicated in 1966. *Photograph by Joe Heidler, J. V. Heidler Co., Inc., n.d.*

York, York County—Beth Israel initially built a religious school, auditorium and social hall on Hollywood Drive in 1962. The original building is faced with multicolored stone and features bas-relief sculptures on the front façade. *Photograph by Julian H. Preisler, 1991*

York, York County—The 1966 hexagonal sanctuary of Beth Israel features magnificent stained glass windows and is known as the "Jewel on the Hill" by local residents. It was recently renovated. *Photograph courtesy of Temple Beth Israel, n.d.*

York, York County—The former 1907 location of Temple Beth Israel on South Beaver Street is now the home of a Catholic church. Some of the Jewish ornamentation has been removed, but the stained glass windows remain. The old synagogue is the only remaining synagogue from the early years of the Jewish community in York. *Sketch courtesy of Gordon Freireich, n.d.*

York, York County—Ohev Sholom Congregation was established in 1902 as an Orthodox congregation and was previously known as the Anshe Hadas which was formed in 1883. Their substantial synagogue at Pershing Avenue and Princess Street was built in 1904. The building was sold and demolished in the late 1960s to facilitate the expansion of the William Penn High School. A new larger synagogue with a religious school was built in 1967 on Eastern Boulevard in Suburban York. *Vintage image courtesy of Gordon Freireich, n.d.*

York, York County—The interior of Ohev Sholom's Pershing Avenue synagogue featured a large sanctuary with an ornate balcony and Ark. Above the Ark was a round stained glass window featuring a beautiful Star of David. *Vintage photograph courtesy of Gordon Freireich, 1932*

York, York County—Ohev Sholom built their new synagogue at 2251 Eastern Boulevard in 1967. The large synagogue featured a round sanctuary and glass cupola topped with a Star of David. The old Ark from the Pershing Avenue synagogue was transferred to the chapel of the new synagogue. Another York congregation, Adas Israel, merged with Ohev Sholom after the new synagogue was built. Because of a decline in membership, the congregation sold the synagogue in 2005 and it was subsequently demolished and replaced by medical offices. Ohev Sholom now shares space with York's Temple Beth Israel. *Photograph by Julian H. Preisler, 1991*

When Ohev Sholom moved from their Eastern Boulevard synagogue, the Ark was dismantled, removed and placed in storage. In 2006, it was re-assembled by local artist Steve March and placed in the lobby of the real estate firm of Elliott Weinstein, a longtime member of Ohev Sholom. The area is now called the "Peace Lobby" and contains historical photos of Ohev Sholom's Pershing Avenue synagogue, as well as architectural elements from a local Lutheran church. It is hoped that one day it will include artifacts representing other religions in York. A painting representing Jacob's Ladder covers the space where the Torahs were originally kept. *Photograph by Elliott Weinstein of Weinstein Realty Advisors, 2013*

# Western Pennsylvania

**Erie** is the fourth largest city in Pennsylvania, located in the northwest of the state along Lake Erie in Erie County. Long a maritime, manufacturing, and industrial center, Erie now has a more diverse economy, including the service sector, tourism and some manufacturing. Erie was established in 1795, but Jewish settlement in the city did not come until the 1840s. Temple Anshe Hesed is the oldest Jewish congregation in the city having been founded in 1846 as a Jewish burial society. A congregation grew out of the burial society and was incorporated in 1862. Anshe Hesed was one of the early members of the new Reform movement and became a member of the Union of American Hebrew Congregations (now Union for Reform Judaism) in 1875. The present synagogue is a well-known landmark in the city that was completed in 1930. Brith Sholom Congregation was established in 1899 as an Orthodox congregation, but now follows the Conservative ritual.

Erie County has several Jewish cemeteries: Anshe Hesed, Ohel Jacob also known as Chesed Shel Emeth, Brith Sholom, Laurel Hill Jewish section, as well as a Jewish Community Council. The nearby community of Corry, also in Erie County, once had a small Jewish community and two synagogues: B'nai Zion Congregation (f. 1854) and Beth Israel Congregation (f. 1882). Little is known when these congregations closed and disbanded and if they ever had permanent buildings. There is also a Jewish cemetery (ca. 1873) in Corry that was owned by the local B'nai B'rith lodge.

**Johnstown,** in Cambria County, is cemented in American history as the location of the disastrous Johnstown Flood (also known as "The Great Flood") of 1889. Johnstown was a city built on iron, steel and coal. The years following the Second World War, marked Johnstown's peak as a steel maker and fabricator. As with most Rust-Belt cities, Johnstown's industry fell into decline and the population shrank.

Johnstown's Jewish community dates to the mid-1850s when there were several Jewish families living in the city. The growth of the local Jewish community did not really occur until the late nineteenth century with the arrival of Jews of Eastern European origin. The first official Jewish organization was Congregation Rodef Sholom chartered in 1889 as an Orthodox congregation. The first synagogue in Johnstown was not built until 1906, when Rodef Sholom dedicated their synagogue at 51 Iron Street (now Walnut Street). The last service in that building was in 1950, when their new synagogue in the Westmont Borough was opened. The old synagogue was demolished in 1962. The second Johnstown synagogue to be built was that of Congregation Ahavath Achim in 1921. This Orthodox congregation was established in 1920.

The synagogue was located at 404 Cedar Street and was in use until 1973. The congregation disbanded due to a decline in membership numbers and the old synagogue was demolished in 1995. Temple Beth Zion, a Reform congregation, was established in Johnstown in 1920. Their first permanent home was located at 416 Vine Street in the large former Nathan Family home which was renovated and remodeled into a synagogue in 1924 to 1926. Temple Beth Zion held their last service there in 1950. Their new synagogue in the Westmont Borough was opened in 1951. The Vine Street location is now the site of a Housing Authority apartment building. Johnstown's Jewish community saw their numbers shrink as industry left Johnstown and many of the local stores and businesses closed. The two remaining congregations merged in 1976 to form Beth Sholom and moved into the former Beth Zion synagogue in Westmont. Though smaller in size than in the past, the Jewish community is active and dedicated to the continuance of Jewish life in Cambria County. It is interesting to note that the grounds of Beth Sholom house the cornerstones from three of the previous four Johnstown synagogues.

**McKeesport** in Allegheny County was once was home to the one of the larger Jewish communities outside of the city of Pittsburgh. German Jews who came to the city starting in 1858 eventually formed a small tight-knit and rather affluent community. By the time the Jews of Eastern European origin began settling in McKeesport in the 1880s, the German Jewish community there had attained a high level of social and economic prosperity. There were a variety of differences between the German Jews and the Eastern European Jews, and by the time these barriers had melted away, most of the German Jewish families had left McKeesport for opportunities in the larger cities. At one time, McKeesport had had a half-dozen or more Jewish congregations, and over the years a variety of Jewish social, charitable and fraternal organizations existed.

The first congregation to be organized was that of the Gemilas Chesed Anshe Ungarn chartered in 1886. The first permanent site for a synagogue in McKeesport was purchased in 1891 and was located at Third and Market. The first purpose-built synagogue in the city was built in 1894 by a group who broke away from Gemilas Chesed because of ethnic and religious differences. The new group, B'nai Israel, built their synagogue on Seventh Avenue. The group did not last more than a year, and the synagogue building was sold to the Slavic Catholic Church. The Russian Jews in the city organized a new congregation, Etz Chaim, around 1895 and built a modest synagogue on Seventh Street in 1897. In 1950, they moved to a new synagogue that still stands on Bailey and Coursin Streets.

The Jews of Galician origin organized their own synagogue, Sfard Anshe Galicia, in 1897 and built a large ornate synagogue on Seventh Street in 1908. Several breakaway congregations existed for a short time during the early years of the community. Another Tree of Life Congregation was chartered in 1898, and, in 1900, ground was broken for a synagogue at Mulberry and Sixth. The congregation lasted until the 1920s, when the building was sold. In 1912, the first congregation in McKeesport to move towards a more modern worship style organized B'nai Israel. Their first synagogue was built in 1923 at 436 Shaw Avenue. They remained in this location until purchasing the former Tree of Life Sfard synagogue in suburban White Oak in 2000. Gemilas Chesed relocated to White Oak in 1963, and the Tree of Life Sfard Congregation relocated to White Oak in 1975 after having merged together in 1973. Though there are no longer any Jewish congregations located in the city of McKeesport, their historic legacy is carried on at Temple B'nai Israel and Gemilas Chesed in White Oak.

**Pittsburgh,** in Allegheny County, means many things to different people. Sports, the steel industry, and famous names such as Mellon, Heinz and Carnegie, come to mind. Pittsburgh has undergone many transformations in its long history—from a military outpost, to a gritty industrial giant, to a clean modern city focused on education, commerce and healthcare.

Jews who had emigrated from Germany to the US first came to the city in the 1830s and 1840s, drawn by the growing industries and business climate that afforded many economic opportunities. The first Jewish religious service was held in 1844; three years later, in 1847, a burial society, Bes Almon or Mourners' House, was formed, and land for a cemetery was purchased on the city's North Side (which was then the City of Allegheny). In 1848, a congregation named Shaare Shamayim was formed out of the burial society. A splinter group formed Beth Israel Congregation in 1852, but reunited a year later. In 1853, the Hebrew Burial society was formed to perform Orthodox burials.

Another split came in 1855 to form the Rodef Shalom Congregation. The congregation received a charter in 1856 and is recognized as the oldest in the city. In 1860, Rodef Shalom and Shaare Shamayim reunited. Rodef Shalom's first synagogue was dedicated in downtown Pittsburgh in 1862. As the Orthodox-oriented Rodef Shalom began to embrace the new Reform Jewish movement espoused by Rabbi Isaac M. Wise, many in the congregation did not embrace the new ideas. In 1864, members of the congregation who desired a more traditional approach to the worship service broke from Rodef Shalom and formed the Orthodox Etz Chaim Congregation. By 1874, Rodef Shalom had fully embraced the Reform movement and joined the Union of American Hebrew Congregations. The Etz chaim later Tree of Life Congregation eventually moved away from orthodoxy and joined the Conservative movement, which was then taking root in the United States. This offered an alternative to Orthodox Judaism, but a less liberal approach than the Reform movement.

Other congregations—many Orthodox in ritual—began forming as more Jews came to Pittsburgh; among them were Jewish immigrants from Eastern Europe and Russia. Other congregations were formed along with Jewish cemeteries, Jewish communal and fraternal organizations, and charitable and professional groups. What is now known as the "Hill District" adjacent to downtown became the center of the immigrant Jewish community, and was Pittsburgh's version of New York City's Lower East Side. Many referred to it as "Jews Hill." A large number of the early Jewish settlers became prominent in commerce and various professions, and anyone familiar with Pittsburgh will remember Kaufmann's Department Store, among others.

Pittsburgh was growing, and the local Jewish community grew along with it. Rodef Shalom's congregation experienced rapid growth in the late nineteenth century, and the original synagogue built in 1862 could no longer meet the needs of the congregation. The congregation built a new synagogue in 1901, choosing to remain at the same physical site where the 1862 synagogue stood. With additional growth, this new synagogue became inadequate only three years later in 1904. As Pittsburgh expanded and many Jewish families gained social and economic prominence, they moved to other emerging areas of the city, such as Oakland, Shadyside, Squirrel Hill and the East End. Synagogues were relocated and new ones built as more people gained the economic ability to afford better housing. In 1907, Rodef Shalom built a new, imposing synagogue on Fifth Avenue in the Oakland area of the city. The new structure was designed by Henry Hornbostel, a noted Pittsburgh architect. Many architectural elements from the old synagogue were incorporated into the new facility. Today the building remains one of Pittsburgh's architectural treasures. The Tree of Life Congregation built their classical style synagogue in 1907 on Craft Avenue on the edge of the Hill District. As the Pittsburgh Jewish community grew, other congregations also built new and beautiful synagogues outside of the original Jewish neighborhood. Congregation B'nai Israel, formed in 1911, built a synagogue designed by Henry Hornbostel in Pittsburgh's East End in 1924. Beth Shalom relocated to Squirrel Hill and built their new large synagogue there in 1923. They were the first congregation to relocate from the Hill District to Squirrel Hill. Poale Zedeck Congregation moved to Squirrel Hill in 1929 and was the first Orthodox synagogue built in the neighborhood.

After the Second World War, new congregations were formed both in the city and its growing suburbs. Squirrel Hill and the East End continued to be active hubs of Jewish activity and residence. Additional synagogues were built, and most Jewish communal facilities followed the Jewish population to Squirrel Hill. Today, it remains a stable center of Jewish life in the city of Pittsburgh. This is unique among Jewish communities in the US, as the vast majority are suburban-oriented rather than urban. Pittsburgh continues to have a very healthy, active and diverse Jewish community. Many of the synagogues and Jewish institutions are well-recognized in the region and the country. There are synagogues of every denomination and type (most with their own buildings), a wide array of Jewish community groups and organizations, a local Jewish newspaper, Jewish schools, historic synagogues and numerous Jewish cemeteries. A beautiful Holocaust Memorial was dedicated in 2013 on the grounds of the Community Day School in Squirrel Hill. Several synagogues in the metro area have Holocaust memorial gardens and Holocaust memorial monuments are to be found in several of the Jewish cemeteries. Jewish Pittsburgh has history, architecture, culture and a vibrant Jewish life.

**Uniontown** is a small city located in southwestern Pennsylvania in Fayette County and dates to 1776. Coal and steel provided for the town's economy until the latter part of the 20th century. Because of the wealth generated during the heyday of industry, Uniontown has a large number of high rise buildings and ornate residences unusual for a city of its size. The year 1882 marks the informal beginning of the Jewish community in Uniontown. Four Jewish families moved to the city, and over the next few decades more Jews settled in Uniontown, including Jewish immigrants with Eastern European origins. It was not until 1904 that a formal congregation was chartered. Temple Israel was organized by about 30 Jewish families who favored the Reform form of worship and ritual. A beautiful synagogue on East Fayette Street was dedicated in 1908. The Orthodox Tree of Life Congregation was organized in either 1902 or 1906. Their first synagogue was a remodeled school house and was dedicated in 1908. As the Jewish community grew, social and fraternal as well as Zionist organizations were formed.

Uniontown's Jewish population was active in all aspects of life in the city. The Standard Club was a well-known Jewish club in the city, and Jewish owned businesses and stores were plentiful. A Young Men's Hebrew Association (later Jewish Community Center) was formed and still exists today. In 1925, the Tree of Life Congregation dedicated their new synagogue on Pennsylvania Avenue. The congregation adopted the Conservative ritual in the 1950s and in the late 1990s became Reform in its ritual and governance. Because of the decline in the local Jewish population, the Tree of Life synagogue was put up for sale in 2013, and the congregation made plans to move to the Jewish Community Center building. Temple Israel sold their impressive 1908 synagogue before 2000 and relocated to the Center. In 2012, the congregation held its last service at the Center, which was a Bat Mitzvah, thus bringing an end to their 100+ year history.

At its beginning, the Jewish Community Center purchased the former Hess Mansion and later built a social hall addition, outdoor swimming pool and playgrounds. Today, the Center also houses a local daycare center. On the grounds there is a very large Holocaust Memorial sculpture and garden which was dedicated in 1982. There are two Jewish cemeteries (one Reform and one Conservative) in nearby Hopwood. Despite the recent decline of the local Jewish population, Jewish life continues on in the city.

There are several former Jewish Communities in Southwest Pennsylvania that deserve mention. Some of these were short lived, and others did not have a building of their own. For some of these communities, it was next to impossible to obtain any information on the synagogues that used to exist there. I felt that it was important to include the following communities. Etna is a small borough in Allegheny County adjacent to Pittsburgh. There once was a Jewish congregation called the Etna & Sharpsburg Jewish Congregation. It was in existence in 1919. McKees Rocks in Allegheny County was the home of Congregation Ahavas Achim which was founded in 1903. Rankin, also in Allegheny County, had an Orthodox congregation that existed from 1908 to about 1956. Congregation Sons of Israel had a synagogue at Grace Street and 2nd Avenue in Rankin that was sold in 1959 and later demolished. Connellsville in Fayette County was once the home of the B'nai Israel Congregation formed in 1897. Beth Jacob Congregation was located in California in Washington County. The congregation was organized around 1915 and their synagogue was located on Liberty Street. An alternate name for the congregation may have been Sons of Jacob. Monongahela, also in Washington County, had a small Orthodox congregation called Tree of Life. The synagogue was located on the first floor of a building in town. When it closed in 1968, the pews from their synagogue were given to Congregation Beth El of the South Hills in suburban Pittsburgh.

Aliquippa, Beaver County—Agudath Achim Congregation was formed in 1909 and chartered in 1919. The congregation purchased a frame house on Church Street in 1921 and remodeled it extensively for use as the synagogue. It was in use until 1959 when the congregation merged with Beth Jacob Congregation of West Aliquippa, established ca. 1915, to form the Aliquippa Jewish Center. *Vintage Image courtesy of Beth Samuel Jewish Center, Ambridge*

Aliquippa, Beaver County—The new Aliquippa Jewish Center was dedicated in 1959 at 2020 Main Street. This synagogue was in use until 1970 when the Center merged with the Beth Samuel Jewish Center in nearby Ambridge. The former synagogue is now used as an office complex. *Photograph by Gail Murray, GaMu Graphic Design, 2013*

Aliquippa, Beaver County—The original design for the new Aliquippa Jewish center was more extensive and bold than what was eventually built. This was not uncommon as congregations often had to modify architect's designs to meet the financial needs of the congregation. *Sketch courtesy of Beth Samuel Jewish Center, Ambridge, n.d.*

Ambridge, Beaver County—Beth Samuel Congregation was chartered in 1914 as Beth Schmuel Congregation (later Beth Samuel). Their first permanent synagogue was located at 463 Maplewood Avenue in Ambridge and was remodeled for use as the synagogue. By 1959 the congregation had outgrown the building and ground was purchased for a new synagogue. The old synagogue is now used as a restaurant. *Photograph by Richard W. Clark, 2013*

Ambridge, Beaver County—Beth Samuel Congregation completed its new synagogue in 1961 at 810 Kennedy Drive in Ambridge. The present congregation is composed of several merged Beaver County congregations: Beth Samuel (Ambridge), Aliquippa Jewish Center (Aliquippa), Beaver Valley United Jewish Community (Beaver Falls) and Agudath Achim (Coraopolis). The congregation is now known as the Beth Samuel Jewish Center and is affiliated with the Reconstructionist movement. *Photograph by Richard W. Clark, 2012*

Beaver Falls, Beaver County—The Agudath Achim Hebrew Congregation was formed in 1904 as an Orthodox congregation. Their yellow brick synagogue was built in 1914 at 5<sup>th</sup> Street and 6<sup>th</sup> Avenue. The congregation, now Conservative, sold their building when the Beaver Valley United Jewish Community Center was built at 2562 Constitution Boulevard in 1959. The old synagogue is now used as a kitchen cabinet workshop. *Photograph By Julian H. Preisler, 2013*

Beaver Falls, Beaver County—The Beaver Valley United Jewish Community Center was chartered in 1957, completed in 1959, and dedicated in 1960. The center housed two sanctuaries, one for the Reform Beth Sholom Congregation, and one for the Conservative Agudath Achim Congregation. Beth Sholom existed from 1960 to 1986 and stemmed from the original Beaver Valley Reform congregation Beth El. The Center was also used by local Jewish community groups. Vintage photograph courtesy of Joel B. Lench, MD, 1985.

Beaver Falls, Beaver County—The Beaver Valley United Jewish Community Center was sold around 1996 and the Agudath Achim continued to meet in rented facilities until 2006 when it effectively merged with Beth Samuel in Ambridge. The building now houses a medical facility. It has been extensively remodeled and there are no traces left to indicate its former use as a synagogue and center. There is a plan to move the memorial plaques to the congregational cemetery. *Photograph by Julian H. Preisler, 2013*

Braddock, Allegheny County—The Orthodox Ahavath Achim Congregation was formed in 1905. Their synagogue is located at 432 6<sup>th</sup> Street and is still open for High Holy Day services each year. The interior remains much as it did when the congregation was large and active. During the rest of the year, the synagogue is locked and secured. *Photograph by Harry "Hank" Katzen, 2008*

Braddock, Allegheny County—The other synagogue in Braddock was the Orthodox Agudath Achim Congregation. Organized in 1894, the bright red brick synagogue is located at 1025 Talbot Avenue and was dedicated in 1902. The "11th Street Shul" was an informal name of the synagogue. Both Braddock congregations merged in 1943 and had hoped to build a new synagogue. *Photograph by Harry "Hank" Katzen, 2008*

Bradford, McKean County—Jewish life in Bradford began in 1879 when the Bradford Hebrew Congregation was organized. Other congregations that existed in Bradford were Beth Israel, Beth Zion, B'nai Israel and Tefares Israel. Temple Beth Zion built their red brick synagogue around 1910 on South Avenue that still stands today. In 1958 the remaining Beth Zion and Beth Israel congregations merged to form Temple Beth El and built a new synagogue. The merged congregation retained the official name of their predecessor congregation, Bradford Hebrew Congregation. *Photograph Courtesy of Linda Halpern Perlman, 2004*

Bradford, McKean County—The interior of the 1910 synagogue of Temple Beth Zion, established in 1880, featured an ornate Ark and Bimah platform, featuring an arch and round stained glass window. *Vintage image courtesy of Todd Halpern, c. 1945*

Bradford, McKean County—The merged congregation now known as Temple Beth El built a large modern synagogue in 1961 on Jackson Avenue. It was in use until 2006 when Temple Beth El, which now had a smaller membership, sold the temple and relocated to a smaller facility. Photograph courtesy of Linda Halpern Perlman, 2004

Bradford, McKean County—Temple Beth El is presently located on Clarence Street in a former church that was remodeled for use as the synagogue. The exterior Tree of Life artwork from the previous temple is now part of the current building's façade. Temple Beth El maintains the Beth Israel Cemetery, the small Tefares Israel Cemetery. There is also a recent Holocaust Memorial at the Beth Israel Cemetery. *Photograph is the property of Lawrence R. Lawson, Temple Beth El, Bradford, PA and is used by permission*

Bradford, McKean County—The sanctuary interior of the present Temple Beth El intentionally mirrors the arrangement of that of its previous location on Jackson Avenue and contains the Ark, lighting and furniture that was housed there in effect recreating the worship space used for many years. *Photograph is the property of Lawrence R. Lawson, Temple Beth El, Bradford, PA and is used by permission*

Brownsville, Fayette County—Ohave Israel Congregation (Lovers of Israel) was established in 1903 or 1907 as an Orthodox congregation. Their synagogue on $2^{nd}$ Street was dedicated in 1919 and cost approximately $45,000. The red brick edifice was elegant with Judaic details and stained glass windows. It appears to reflect the relative prosperity of the former Jewish Community. Ohave Israel disbanded in 1969 as industry left the area and the Jewish population declined. The synagogue is now used as a business, but has been maintained and retains the beautiful stained glass windows. Some artifacts, torahs and memorial plaques are now located in the chapel of Congregation Beth El in suburban Pittsburgh. A small Jewish cemetery is located in South Brownsville. *Photograph by Jane McAnn Walsh, 2007*

Butler, Butler County—B'nai Abraham Congregation is an Independent/Egalitarian congregation established in 1903. The congregation's first synagogue at 201 Fifth Avenue was dedicated in 1914 and still stands today. The present red brick modern synagogue was built in 1956 as an addition to the large mansion that was in use by the congregation. It is located at 519 Main Street and is noted for its exterior artwork and stained glass windows in the sanctuary. *Photograph courtesy of Cantor Michal Gray-Schaffer and Kim Csonka of B'nai Abraham Congregation, 2013*

Butler, Butler County—The former location of B'nai Abraham built in 1914 is today used as a church. It is a yellow/beige brick building with stained glass windows and simple Gothic period detailing. *Photograph courtesy of Cantor Michal Gray-Schaffer and Kim Csonka of B'nai Abraham Congregation, 2013*

Canonsburg, Washington County—Jews settled in Canonsburg as early as 1900. A Jewish congregation was organized around 1905 as B'nai Israel and later known as the Canonsburg Hebrew Association. When the congregation was formally organized, the name Tree of Life Congregation was chosen. Their only synagogue was dedicated in 1915 on Ashland Avenue. The congregation disbanded in the 1960s due to a decline in the local Jewish population, and the synagogue building was demolished in 1980. Canonsburg was once home to the well-known Canonsburg Pottery Company. *Vintage image courtesy of Arnold W. Cushner. n.d.*

Carnegie, Allegheny County—Ahavas Achim Congregation is a Traditional congregation organized informally in 1896 and chartered in 1903. The original synagogue at 204 Broadway burned in 1934, and a new synagogue was built at 500 Chestnut Street in 1937. An L-shaped addition was built in 1964 to the front and side of the building. The Sanctuary today appears just as it was when built in 1937. *Photographs courtesy of Rick D'Loss and Congregation Ahavas Achim, 2008*

Charleroi, Washington County—Rodef Shalom Congregation was organized in 1907. In 1925 the congregation built their brick synagogue at 425 Washington Avenue. It contained stained glass windows throughout and symbols of the Torah on the façade. The congregation disbanded and closed sometime before 2007. The congregation may have also been known as Beth Israel at some point in its history. Some of the stained glass windows were removed when the synagogue closed and were installed in the Sanctuary at Beth El Congregation in suburban Pittsburgh. *Photograph by Jay W. Mahoney, 2007*

Clairton, Allegheny County— Congregation B'nai Abraham was an Orthodox congregation incorporated in 1908. Their only synagogue was housed in a former church on Waddell Avenue near 3rd Street and was remodeled for use a Jewish house of worship. As the building did not face east, the front entrance was blocked and the Ark placed there. This became the front of the sanctuary and worshipers had to enter the synagogue through the kitchen door. When industry left the city, the Jewish population declined, and the synagogue disbanded. *Vintage image courtesy of Marian Ungar Davis, n.d.*

Clearfield, Clearfield County— Temple Beth Shalom was organized in 1917 and may also have been known as B'nai Levi and/or House of Jacob. Their only synagogue was located in a former Pennsylvania Telephone Company building at 110 East Locust Street and remodeled for use as the synagogue. A stained glass window with a Star of David was placed above the entrance. The congregation closed around 2010 and merged with Congregation Brit Shalom in State College. Historical and religious artifacts were moved to Brit Shalom. There is a small Jewish section of the municipal cemetery. *Photograph by Harry "Hank" Katzen, 2008*

Clearfield, Clearfield County—It is not known when the congregation began worshiping in the former Pennsylvania Telephone Company building which was built ca. 1910. It is a substantial building, and at one time the congregation's membership must have been significant enough to warrant the use of a larger structure. *Photograph by Harry "Hank" Katzen, 2008*

Clearfield, Clearfield County—The Star of David stained glass window above the entrance to the former synagogue appears to be still in place in 2013. The building is now home to the Clearfield Arts Studio Theater. *Photograph by Harry "Hank" Katzen, 2008*

Coraopolis, Allegheny County—Ahavath Sholom congregation was formed sometime prior to the 1930s. Various locations were used for worship and religious school until a former church at Vance and Fleming Streets was purchased in the 1950s and remodeled for use as a synagogue. Due to the decline in the Jewish population in Coraopolis, Ahavath Sholom merged with Beth Samuel of Ambridge in 1982. The former church turned synagogue now serves as a church again. *Vintage image courtesy of Beth Samuel Congregation, Ambridge, n.d.*

Donora, Washington County—Oheb Sholom Congregation was an Orthodox synagogue located at Thompson Avenue and 2nd Street. Established ca. 1911, the synagogue was built before 1917 and closed around 1993 due to a decline in the local Jewish population. The building is now home to the Mon Valley Youth and Teen Association. The Eldora Cemetery in Donora established by Oheb Sholom is still in use. *Photograph by Becky Cappelli, 2007*

1 Altoona, Blair County—Sanctuary interior of Temple Beth Israel. *Photograph by Don Clippinger and courtesy of Temple Beth Israel, 2013*

2 Ambridge, Beaver County—Sanctuary interior of the Beth Samuel Jewish Center. *Photograph by Gail Murray, GaMu Graphic Design, 2013*

3  Butler, Butler County—
Sanctuary interior of B'nai
Abraham Congregation. *Photograph
by Cantor Michal Gray-Schaffer
and courtesy of B'nai Abraham
Congregation, 2013*

4  Carnegie, Allegheny County—Sanctuary interior of the Ahavas Achim Congregation. The interior
is just as it was when it was built in 1937. *Photograph by Richard D'Loss and courtesy of Ahavas Achim, 2008*

5  DuBois, Clearfield County—Sanctuary interior of the Sons of Israel Congregation.
*Photograph by Harry "Hank" Katzen, 2013*

6  Harrisburg, Dauphin County—Sanctuary interior of the new Chisuk Emuna synagogue.
*Photograph by Robin B. Schuldenfrei, CAVU Creative, 2013*

7 Harrisburg, Dauphin County—Sanctuary interior of Kesher Israel Congregation. *Photograph by Daniel Grabenstein and courtesy of Kesher Israel, 2013*

8 Harrisburg, Dauphin County— Sanctuary interior of Temple Ohev Sholom. *Photograph by Rabbi Peter Kessler and courtesy of Ohev Sholom, 2013*

9 Harrisburg, Dauphin County—Interior of the Lehrman Chapel at Temple Ohev Sholom. The Ark and stained glass windows were designed by David Ascalon of the Ascalon Studios. *Photograph by Rabbi Peter Kessler and courtesy of Ohev Sholom, 2013*

10 Indiana, Indiana County—Sanctuary interior of Beth Israel Synagogue. *Photograph by Hannah Maia Frishberg, 2013*

11 Johnstown, Cambria County—Sanctuary interior of Beth Sholom Congregation. *Photograph by Barry Rudel and courtesy of the Johnstown Jewish community, 2013*

12 Lock Haven, Clinton County—Sanctuary interior of Beth Yehuda Synagogue. *Photograph by Richard W. Clark, 2013*

13  Lock Haven, Clinton County—Detail of one of ten exterior mosaic murals on the façade of the Beth Yehuda Synagogue. Artist unknown. *Photograph by Richard W. Clark, 2013*

14  Meadville, Crawford County—Sanctuary and social hall interior of the Meadville Jewish Community Center & Synagogue. *Photograph by Jane Ellen Nickell, Chaplain, Allegheny College, 2013*

15  Mechanicsburg, Cumberland County—Sanctuary interior of Temple Beth Shalom of Greater Harrisburg. *Photograph by Ira Beckerman of Beth Shalom, 2013*

16  Middletown, Dauphin County—Sanctuary interior of the historic B'nai Jacob Synagogue. *Photograph by Jack E. Kapp, Kapptured Moments Photography, Philadelphia, 2013*

17 Monroeville, Allegheny County—Sanctuary interior of Temple David, a Pittsburgh area Reform congregation. *Photograph by Julie Cohen and courtesy of Temple David, 2013*

18 Mount Carmel, Northumberland County—Sanctuary interior of the former Tifereth Israel Synagogue taken prior to the sale of the synagogue, pre 1986. *Photograph courtesy of Ted Matlow and Howard L. Ross*

19  New Castle, Lawrence County—Colorful 1950s mosaic tile mural at the entrance to the Hadar Israel Congregation synagogue, which was built as the Tifereth Israel Congregation. *Photograph by Julian H. Preisler, 2013*

20  Oil City, Venango County—Sanctuary interior of the Tree of Life Synagogue. *Photograph by Linda Halpern Perlman, 2004*

21 Cheswick/Indiana Township, Allegheny County—Sanctuary interior of Adat Shalom Synagogue (B'nai Israel-Beth Jacob) in suburban Pittsburgh. *Photograph by Dr. Bernard D. Newman, 2013*

22 Jefferson Hills, Allegheny County—Sanctuary of the Beth Israel Center in the South Hills of suburban Pittsburgh. *Photograph by Rachel Weinblum, Beth Israel Center, 2013*

23  Pittsburgh, Allegheny County—Sanctuary interior of Congregation Beth Shalom. After a devastating fire in 1996, the synagogue and sanctuary were rebuilt. *Photograph by Toni Miga, 2013*

24  Pittsburgh, Allegheny County—Sanctuary interior of the former B'nai Israel Synagogue in the East Liberty neighborhood. It is listed as a local historic landmark, but the sanctuary is currently vacant. *Photograph by Hans Jonas and courtesy of Jonas Photography, Pittsburgh, 1997*

25  Pittsburgh/Wilkins Township, Allegheny County—Sanctuary interior of the Parkway Jewish Center—Congregation Sha'are HaShamayim in the eastern suburbs of Pittsburgh. *Photograph by Gail Levine and courtesy of the Parkway Jewish Center, 2013*

26  Pittsburgh, Allegheny County—Sanctuary interior of the Poale Zedeck Synagogue in Pittsburgh's Squirrel Hill neighborhood. *Photograph by Richard W. Clark, 2013*

27  Pittsburgh, Allegheny County—Sanctuary interior of Rodef Shalom's historic 1907 synagogue.
*Photograph courtesy of Lauren Wolcott and Rodeph Shalom, 2011*

28  Mount Lebanon, Allegheny County—Interior of the main sanctuary at Temple Emanuel of the
South Hills in suburban Pittsburgh. *Photograph by Saralouise Reis and courtesy of Temple Emanuel, 2013*

29  Washington, Washington County—Interior of the main sanctuary at the present Beth Israel Congregation. *Photograph by Marilyn Posner and courtesy of Beth Israel, 2013*

30  White Oak, Allegheny County—Sanctuary interior of Temple B'nai Israel in suburban Pittsburgh. *Photograph courtesy of Dick Leffel and B'nai Israel*

31  Williamsport, Lycoming County—Sanctuary interior of Ohev Sholom Congregation. *Photograph by Richard W. Clark, 2013*

32  Williamsport, Lycoming County—Exterior view of several of the dozen stained glass windows at Ohev Sholom Congregation. *Photograph by Richard W. Clark, 2013*

DuBois, Clearfield County—Sons of Israel is a Reform congregation incorporated in 1894, originally as an Orthodox congregation. The present synagogue at Morrison Street and Webber Avenue was purchased in 1911 and was formerly a church. It was remodeled for use as a synagogue, and a "Community Room" addition was built in 1926. When the synagogue in nearby Punxsutawney closed, the memorial tablets were moved to the DuBois synagogue. There is a Jewish cemetery in DuBois. *Photograph by Harry "Hank" Katzen, 2013*

Duquesne, Allegheny County—Beth Jacob was an Orthodox congregation organized in 1904. Their brick synagogue was built at 17 South 2nd Street in 1923. It was of good size with an elegant three-arched entrance. The congregation closed sometime prior to the 1990s. It once had beautiful leaded glass windows which were later removed and the windows boarded up. *Photograph by Mark Gordon, 2008*

65

Ellwood City, Lawrence County—Ellwood City is located in both Lawrence and Beaver counties and once had a sizable Jewish community. The Tree of Life Congregation was a Conservative synagogue organized around 1900 as an Orthodox congregation. Their first synagogue, built in 1910, was located at Wayne Avenue and 7th Street, and is now a church. The synagogue had a balcony where the women of the congregation sat during services. The congregation eventually moved away from Orthodoxy and became affiliated with the Conservative movement. *Photograph by Julian H. Preisler, 2013*

Ellwood City, Lawrence County—In 1952, a new synagogue for the Tree of Life Congregation was built at Beatty Street and Sims in the Ewing Park section of town. A large addition was constructed later in that decade. The congregation closed in 1989, and the building was given to the Ellwood City Hospital. It is now home to the Visiting Nurses Association. *Photograph by Julian H. Preisler, 2013*

Ellwood City, Lawrence County—The former Tree of Life synagogue still retains much of the exterior Jewish art on the side of the building and at the front entrance. The sanctuary space still has the large built in Ark, though the Torahs were, of course, removed when the congregation closed. *Photograph by Julian H. Preisler, 2013*

Erie, Erie County—Temple Anshe Hesed is a Reform congregation first established as a burial society in 1846 and later incorporated as a congregation in 1862. It became one of the initial members of the Reform movement in 1875. The present landmark synagogue at 930 Liberty Street was built in 1930. In 1959, the Currick Memorial Building was added with additional classrooms, a chapel and library. An art gallery was added in the 1970s along with renovations to the Sanctuary. *Photograph courtesy of Temple Anshe Hesed, n.d.*

Erie, Erie County—This beautiful sketch by Timothy McLaughlin, 2009, shows the entire Anshe Hesed synagogue with its hexagonal sanctuary and additions. *Courtesy of Temple Anshe Hesed.*

Erie, Erie County—Brith Sholom Congregation was established in 1899 as an Orthodox congregation. In 1954, a synagogue and center was built at 3207 State Street. A larger Sanctuary was built in 1956. Several years ago the congregation entered into a building agreement with the Jefferson Educational Society. The Society uses the southern wing of the synagogue complex for educational seminars, lectures and other events to promote intellectual growth and community progress in Erie County. Brith Sholom continues to use the synagogue, sanctuary and northern wing. *Photograph by Nan Patterson, 2007*

Glassport, Allegheny County—B'nai Israel Congregation was an Orthodox congregation organized in 1906. Their synagogue at 523 Ohio Avenue was built in 1916 and now appears to be empty. The congregation sold the building and disbanded in 1976 due to a decline in the local Jewish population. *Photograph by Julian H. Preisler, 2013*

Greensburgh, Westmoreland County—Congregation Emanue-El Israel is the result of the merger in 1981 of the Conservative B'nai Israel and the Reform Emanu-El. Temple Emanu-El was formed in 1945 and their synagogue was dedicated in 1951. It was built of Ohio stone and designed by Pittsburgh architect, Philip Friedman. In 1981, it became the home of the merged congregation. In 1967, Congregation Chevra Sholom in Jeannette merged with B'nai Israel. Memorial plaques from the former B'nai Israel and Chevra Sholom were moved to the present synagogue. Each congregation had its own cemetery in Greensburg located adjacent to each other. *Photograph by Julian H. Preisler, 2012*

Greensburgh—Westmoreland County—B'nai Israel was established in 1890 as an Orthodox congregation. Their former synagogue, ca. 1914, still stands at Ludwick Street and North Hamilton Avenue. B'nai Israel later became Conservative, and when they merged with what was then Temple Emanu-El, the synagogue was sold. The synagogue is in poor condition and is used as a repair shop. *Photograph by Mark Gordon, 2007*

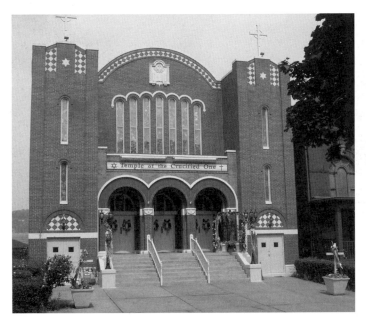

Homestead, Allegheny County—The Rodef Sholom Homestead Hebrew Congregation was organized in 1894 and their first synagogue burned in 1911. A new synagogue at 329 East 10th Avenue was dedicated in 1914. The congregation closed in 1992 and there is a Homestead Chapel at Beth Shalom Congregation in Pittsburgh in memory of the former Homestead synagogue. The original pews and stained glass windows from the former synagogue, now a church, remain. *Photograph by Mark Gordon, 2005*

Indiana, Indiana County—Beth Israel is a Reform congregation located at Washington Street and South 5<sup>th</sup> Street in Indiana County. The modern red brick synagogue was first used for services in 1952 and it was at this time that the name was changed from the Hebrew Unity Congregation to Beth Israel. The congregation was officially established in October 1916. In 1949, a Beth Israel section of Oakland Cemetery was created. *Photograph by Julian H. Preisler, 2013*

Jeannette, Westmoreland County—The Chevra Sholom Congregation was a former Orthodox congregation whose synagogue at 600 Gaskill Street was built in 1939. The synagogue was built in memory of Anna R. Gross. The congregation merged with Congregation B'nai Israel in Greensburg in 1979. The memorial plaques from the congregation were moved to B'nai Israel's synagogue in Greensburgh, and when B'nai Israel merged with Temple Emanu-El in 1981, the plaques were once again relocated to their new home. The Jeannette synagogue is now a church. *Photograph by Julian H. Preisler, 2007*

Johnstown, Cambria County—
Ahavath Achim was an Orthodox
congregation founded in 1920 by
former members of Johnstown's
Rodef Sholom Congregation. Their
synagogue was located at 404
Cedar Street and built in 1921. The
building was demolished in 1995.
The congregation disbanded in 1973.
*Vintage image courtesy of the Rauh Jewish
Archive of the Senator John Heinz History
Center, Pittsburgh, n.d.*

Johnstown, Cambria County—The
interior of Johnstown's Ahavath
Achim synagogue featured a
traditional arrangement of the Ark
and reader's platform. *Photograph
courtesy of Beth Sholom and the
Johnstown Area Heritage Association, n.d.*

Johnstown, Cambria County—Beth Sholom Congregation was formed by the merger in 1976 of the two remaining Johnstown congregations, Beth Zion and Rodeph Sholom. The present Beth Sholom synagogue completed in 1951 was designed by Alexander Sharove. It is faced with multicolored stone and has a large stone menorah sculpture on the façade. A. Raymond Katz, a noted artist, designed the windows at Beth Sholom. His murals, windows and bas-relief sculptures can be found on two hundred American synagogues. *Photograph By Barry Rudel, 2013*

Johnstown, Cambria County—The cornerstones of several of Johnstown synagogues are incorporated into the entrance area of the Beth Sholom synagogue. Rodof Sholem 1905, Ahavath Achim, 1921 and Beth Zion 1950 which is the present Beth Sholom synagogue. *Photograph by Barry Rudel, 2013*

Johnstown, Cambria County—The architectural drawings for the planned Beth Zion synagogue, 1950, accurately reflect what was eventually built. This was often not the case and the size and architecture depended on the financial means of a congregation. *Sketch courtesy of Beth Sholom Congregation and the Johnstown Area Heritage Association, n.d.*

Johnstown, Cambria County—Temple Beth Zion was Johnstown's Reform synagogue and was established in 1920. Their first permanent home was located at 416 Vine Street in the large former home of the Nathan family. The residence was renovated and remodeled into a synagogue between 1924 and 1926. The cornerstone of Beth Zion's new synagogue in Westmont Borough was laid in 1950. *Vintage image courtesy of Beth Sholom Congregation and the Johnstown Area Heritage Association, n.d.*

Johnstown, Cambria County—
Rodeph Sholom was established as
an Orthodox congregation in 1889
and was the first Jewish congregation
in Johnstown. The first synagogue
to be built in Johnstown was not
constructed until 1905-1906 when
Rodef Sholom opened their synagogue
at 51 Iron Street (now Walnut Street).
The building featured elegant
details and stained glass windows.
That building no longer stands.
*Vintage image courtesy of Beth Sholom
Congregation and the Johnstown Area
Heritage Association, circa 1940s*

Johnstown, Cambria County—Rodeph Sholom followed the trend of the Jewish community movement to Westmont Borough, and in 1950 they built their new modern synagogue at 100 Dartmouth Avenue just around the corner from the new Beth Zion. The architect was also Alexander Sharove. When the two remaining synagogues in the city merged, the Dartmouth Avenue synagogue was sold around 1978 to a local school district. It is now the home of the Ferndale Area Elementary School. *Photograph by Barry Rudel, 2013*

Kane, McKean County—Beth Jacob was a small Orthodox congregation established around 1915. Their former synagogue, built around 1918, and located at 39 Kinzua Road is now used as a warehouse. The congregation closed around 1960. There was a small Jewish cemetery in Kane, but the land was sold and the graves moved, most likely, to Bradford. *Photograph is the property of Lawrence R. Lawson, Temple Beth El, Bradford, PA and is used by permission*

Kittaning, Armstrong County—Knesseth Israel was formed in 1908 probably as an Orthodox congregation. Their former synagogue located at 599 North Water Street was dedicated June 4, 1954. The congregation closed around 1991, as there were no longer enough Jews in the city to sustain an active congregation. The synagogue was purchased by First United Methodist Church and rededicated October 27, 1991 as their Covenant Center. *Photograph By Julian H. Preisler, 2013*

Kittaning, Armstrong County—When the Knesseth Israel synagogue was sold and became the Covenant Center of the First United Methodist Church, the church took steps to maintain most of the Jewish symbols, windows and design on the exterior as a tribute to the former Jewish community in Kittaning. At one point in time there was a large metal menorah sculpture on the roof above the entrance to the synagogue. *Photograph by Julian H. Preisler, 2013*

Latrobe, Westmoreland County—The first Jewish resident of Latrobe was Henry Fellheimer who arrived in 1854. An Orthodox congregation, Beth Israel, was organized in 1906, and their first synagogue was built in 1907 on Miller Street, in the area known as "Jew Town." The present synagogue, which is Conservative, is located at 414 Weldon Street and was dedicated in 1954. Comedian Jackie Mason was an ordained Rabbi and served this congregation in the early 1960s. *Photograph by Peter Radunzel, 2011*

Latrobe, Westmoreland County—Beth Israel's synagogue is a low Mid-Century Modern building faced in brown, beige and yellow brick. On the façade there is a bas-relief sculpture with the Ten Commandments, Stars of David and the name Beth Israel. It is a simple structure that in many ways is typical of the functional synagogues built in many small towns during the middle of the twentieth century. *Photograph by Julian H. Preisler, 2011*

Masontown, Fayette County—Beth El Synagogue was established around the turn of the twentieth century. Their former synagogue is located at 9 South Washington Street. When the congregation closed in the 1950s the building was given to the borough for use as a library. A new library was recently built and the former synagogue is now used as a church. There is a Jewish cemetery, Holy Society Jewish Cemetery, in nearby Hopwood. *Photograph by Julian H. Preisler, 2013*

McKeesport, Allegheny County—Temple B'nai Israel was formed in 1912, by those who preferred a more modern approach to Jewish worship. Their synagogue was dedicated in 1923 on Shaw Avenue and was one of the most elegant synagogues to date built in the city at a cost of around $125,000. B'nai Israel was originally Conservative, but became Reform in 1940. B'nai Israel sold the Shaw Avenue temple in 2000 and purchased the existing synagogue of the Tree of Life Sfard Congregation in White Oak. The church that purchased the synagogue has restored and renovated the building with historical accuracy in keeping with its former life as a synagogue. *Photograph by Julian H. Preisler, 2013*

McKeesport, Allegheny County—The Tree of Life Congregation originally known as Etz Chaim was established in the 1940s and traces its origin to the Tree of Life Congregation that was chartered in 1898. Their synagogue was built around 1950 at Bailey and Coursin Street, and, in 1974, became the McKeesport Little Theater. *Vintage image courtesy of Temple B'nai Israel, White Oak, n.d.*

*Above:* McKeesport, Allegheny County—The farewell service in Gemilas Chesed's Seventh Street synagogue was October 30, 1960. The members of the congregation were now centered in suburban White Oak and, as an Orthodox congregation, the members needed to be within walking distance of the synagogue. The building was sold and demolished in 1963. The interior of the synagogue contained a horseshoe-shaped balcony, elaborate Ark and large stained glass windows. *Photograph courtesy of Ruth Gordon and Gemilas Chesed Congregation, n.d.*

*Opposite above:* McKeesport, Allegheny County—The Tree of Life Congregation and the Sfard Congregation (f. 1897) merged in 1973, and two years later moved to their new synagogue on Cypress Drive in nearby White Oak. In 2000, they sold their building to Temple B'nai Israel, which was relocating from McKeesport to White Oak. Their former synagogue, which became the McKeesport Little Theater, has been greatly modified and the only trace of its former use is the menorah carving that is visible and was part of the entrance to the synagogue. *Photograph by Richard W. Clark, 2013*

*Opposite below:* McKeesport, Allegheny County—The Gemilas Chesed Congregation is an Orthodox congregation that was formerly located in McKeesport. The congregation was chartered in 1886 as Gemilas Chesed Anshe Ungarn and their first purpose built synagogue was dedicated in 1904 on Seventh Street. It served the congregation until 1960 when the building was sold and the congregation relocated to suburban White Oak. The synagogue was one of the more elaborate synagogues built in McKeesport. *Photograph courtesy of Ruth Gordon and Gemilas Chesed Congregation, c. 1959*

Meadville, Crawford County—With roots going back to 1866, the present Jewish congregation was organized in the 1930s and was known as the Meadville Hebrew Society. Efforts to build a synagogue began in 1952. The first service in the present synagogue at 379 Park Avenue took place for the High Holy Days of 1955. It now a small but active synagogue known as the Jewish Community Center. The synagogue also serves as a home for Allegheny College Hillel. There is a local Jewish cemetery that may have been used as early as 1880. *Photograph by Jane Ellen Nickell, Chaplain, Allegheny College, 2013*

Midland, Beaver County—Former Orthodox congregation established in 1915 and chartered in 1918 as of Sons of Israel Congregation. In 1927, a synagogue at 7th Street and Beaver Avenue was dedicated and the name B'nai Israel adopted. In 1946, the congregation adopted the more liberal Conservative ritual. The congregation no longer exists, and the synagogue has since been demolished. *Vintage image Courtesy of the Rauh Jewish Archives at the Senator John Heinz History Center, Pittsburgh, n.d.*

Monessen, Westmoreland County—Temple Beth Am is a result of the merger of Keneseth Israel (f. 1903) of Monessen and Rodef Shalom Congregation (f. 1908) of nearby Charleroi. Jewish religious services were held in Monessen as early as 1903. The present synagogue at 1000 Watkins Avenue was dedicated in 1954 for Keneseth Israel and replaced their synagogue from 1911 that was located in downtown Monessen. The Temple Beth Am/Keneseth Israel Cemetery contains a Holocaust Memorial. *Photograph courtesy of Becky Cappelli, 2007*

Monessen, Westmoreland County—The members of Temple Beth Am remain dedicated to continuing Jewish life in Monessen, even though their numbers have diminished. The synagogue is beige brick with beige and brown stone on the façade. There is a permanent Chanukah menorah on the wall of the synagogue to the left of the entrance. *Photograph courtesy of Becky Cappelli, 2007*

Monessen, Westmoreland County—The sanctuary interior of Temple Beth Am appears much as it was when built for the Knesseth Israel Congregation in 1954. *Photograph courtesy of Jack Bergstein and Temple Beth Am, 2013*

Monessen, Westmoreland County—A 1954 photograph shows the sanctuary of the Knesseth Israel synagogue right after it was built and before the addition of the menorah sculptures on either side of the Ark, as well as the Yahrzeit memorial plaques at the front of the sanctuary. *Vintage photograph courtesy of Jack Bergstein and Temple Beth Am*

Monessen, Westmoreland County—A 1954 close-up view of the Ark at the front of Knesseth Israel's sanctuary at the time the synagogue was completed. *Vintage photograph courtesy of Jack Bergstein and Temple Beth Am*

Monroeville, Allegheny County—Temple David is a Reform congregation established in 1958 in the eastern suburbs of Pittsburgh. The synagogue at 4415 Northern Pike was built in 1960 or 1961 with major additions and renovations taking place in 1981 and 2002. *Photograph By Julie Cohen and courtesy of Temple David, 2013*

Monroeville, Allegheny County—Temple David's renovated and expanded entrance area. Temple David is unique in that eight of their religious school confirmands went on to become rabbis. *Photographs By Julie Cohen and courtesy of Temple David, 2013*

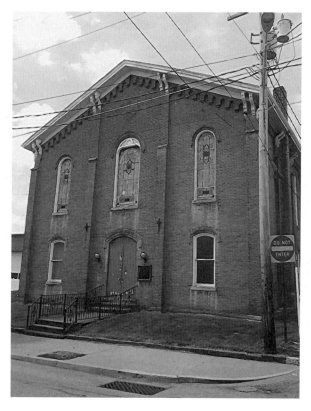

Mount Pleasant, Westmoreland County—A Jewish congregation was organized in the 1880s, became the Tree of Life Congregation in 1900, and was incorporated in 1923. Their former synagogue is located at 26 South Church Street. It was built as a church in 1877 and remodeled for use as the synagogue in 1938. The congregation was active in 1978, but closed sometime thereafter. The building is now owned by the borough and used for storage. The Jewish-themed stained glass windows appear to remain. *Photograph by Michael J. Meehan, n.d.*

New Castle, Lawrence County—Tifereth Israel was incorporated in 1894 as an Orthodox congregation, though religious services were held in members' homes in New Castle, beginning in 1870. The Jews in New Castle at one time formed a large part of the merchant class in town. Their first synagogue was dedicated in 1909. Tifereth Israel built a large modern synagogue in 1957 at 403 East Moody Avenue. In 1998, the Conservative Tifereth Israel and the Reform Temple Israel merged to form Congregation Hadar Israel. *Photograph by Julian H. Preisler, 2013*

New Castle, Lawrence County—When the two Jewish congregations merged, they decided to sell the Temple Israel building and use Tifereth Israel's building. After the merger, extensive renovations were undertaken to renovate and update the synagogue. Among the additions to the building were numerous beautiful stained glass windows in varying shapes and sizes. *Photograph by Julian H. Preisler, 2013*

New Castle, Lawrence County—The exterior of Hadar Israel's synagogue features a number of large Judaic symbols including the Star of David, a Torah scroll, and the metal menorah that once graced the entrance of Temple Israel down the street. *Photograph by Julian H. Preisler, 2013*

New Castle, Lawrence County—Temple Israel was a Reform congregation that was located at East Moody Avenue and Highland Street. Temple Israel organized in 1926 and built their synagogue in 1927. The buff brick and stone temple featured many stained glass windows and a stone menorah sculpture above the entrance. In 1998, the congregation merged with the former Tifereth Israel Congregation to form Temple Hadar Israel. The old Temple Israel building now houses a local church. *Photograph by Julian H. Preisler, 2013*

New Kensington, Westmoreland County—Beth Jacob was formally organized in 1908 as an Orthodox congregation. It later became Conservative. Their yellow brick synagogue was dedicated in 1926 at 1040 Kenneth Avenue. In 1964, a modern addition was built and the sanctuary was renovated. Due to a decline in the local Jewish population, the congregation merged with B'nai Israel of the East End in Pittsburgh to form Adat Shalom in 1995. The exterior artwork, some stained glass windows, and artifacts from Beth Jacob were transferred to Adat Shalom's new building. The former synagogue is now home to a church. *Photograph courtesy of Dr. Bernard D. Newman and Adat Shalom Congregation, 1995*

New Kensington, Westmoreland County—The sanctuary of Beth Jacob's synagogue was an elegant worship space with a balcony, beautiful wooden Ark and pulpit, stained glass window above the ark, and a large brass chandelier. *Photograph courtesy of Dr. Bernard D. Newman and Adat Shalom Congregation, 1995*

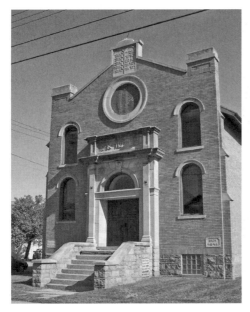

Northern Cambria, Cambria County—B'nai Israel was an Orthodox synagogue located on Maple Avenue. It was built in 1925, dedicated in 1927, and closed in 1968. The building was then given to the borough of Barnesboro, but sat empty. Restoration by the Coal Country Hangout Youth Center began around 2010. It will be used by the United Way, Susquehanna Historical Society, and other agencies. Students from the local high school have researched the history of the building and Jewish families that once lived in the borough. Barnesboro and nearby Spangler merged in 2000 to become one borough of Northern Cambria. Barnesboro was the smallest town in Pennsylvania to have an actual synagogue. *Photograph by Justin Greggi, 2011*

Northern Cambria, Cambria County—B'nai Israel was a very active congregation in its heyday, and Barnesboro's Jews were well respected merchants in town. Barnesboro (Now Northern Cambria) was the smallest town in Pennsylvania to have an actual synagogue. The building was simple in design, but had impressive architectural details on the façade. *Photograph by Marilyn Washington, 2007*

Oil City, Venango County—The Tree of Life Congregation was established sometime prior to 1897 when their first synagogue was built at Plummer and Center Street. The congregation, which was originally Orthodox, outgrew their original synagogue and also later adopted the Conservative ritual. The present-day synagogue, located at 316 West 1st Street, was built in 1957. It is a low modern building with clerestory windows above the sanctuary. A breakaway congregation, Shearith Israel (name uncertain), existed for two years sometime in the early twentieth century. They did not have their own building, but did establish their own cemetery, Sage Run Jewish Cemetery. *Photograph Courtesy of Penny Minnick 2007*

Oil City, Venango County—The Jewish population of Oil City today is extremely small, and an agreement was recently made between the Tree of Life Congregation and the local YMCA for use of portions of the synagogue building. The congregation has a cemetery that is actually located in Titusville, which is in Crawford County. The Mt. Zion Jewish Cemetery (1870) is located in the city of Franklin in Venango County. It was established solely as a Jewish burial ground without a Jewish congregation. *Photograph is the property of Lawrence R. Lawson, Temple Beth El, Bradford, PA, and is used by permission*

Oil City, Venango County—The original synagogue of the Tree of Life Congregation was an impressive brick building with twin domes and a large stained glass window over the entrance featuring a Star of David. The old synagogue was sold to a church and later demolished. *Vintage image courtesy of Todd Halpern, n.d.*

Cheswick/Indiana Township, Allegheny County—Adat Shalom was formed in 1995 by the merger of B'nai Israel Congregation of East Liberty (Pittsburgh) and Beth Jacob Congregation of New Kensington. The present synagogue was formerly the Divine Providence Academy built in 1965 and purchased in 1995. The building was remodeled and dedicated as a synagogue the following year. Adat Shalom is actually located in Indiana Township, but has a Cheswick mailing address. *Photograph by Dr. Bernard D. Newman and courtesy of Adat Shalom, 2013*

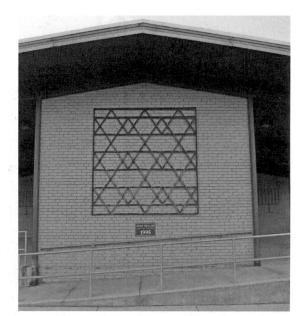

Cheswick/Indiana Township, Allegheny County—Exterior artwork and stained glass windows (over 100 years old) from the former Beth Jacob in New Kensington were incorporated into the new synagogue, as were religious items and artifacts from the historic B'nai Israel synagogue in Pittsburgh. *Photograph by Dr. Bernard D. Newman and courtesy of Adat Shalom, 2013*

Pittsburgh, Allegheny County—Adath Jeshurun Congregation is a former synagogue located at Margaretta Street (now East Liberty Boulevard) and North St. Claire Street in the East Liberty neighborhood of Pittsburgh. Founded in 1916, the synagogue was built in 1924. In 1978, Congregation Cneseth Israel, another Orthodox congregation (f. 1905) in the East End, merged with Adath Jeshurun. The congregation relocated to suburban Monroeville in 1996, but the congregation closed in 2002 due to low membership. The former synagogue in East Liberty is now a church. *Photograph by Julian H. Preisler, 2011*

Pittsburgh, Allegheny County—The sanctuary of the former Adath Jeshurun synagogue featured a women's balcony (typical of older Orthodox synagogues), a large wooden Ark and the traditional Sephardic arrangement of the reader's platform. The Ark was moved to the new building in Monroeville. *Vintage image courtesy of the Rauh Jewish Archive of the Senator John Heinz History Center, Pittsburgh, n.d.*

Mount Lebanon, Allegheny County—Beth El Congregation of the South Hills is a Conservative congregation located at 1900 Cochran Road in suburban Pittsburgh. Founded in 1916, their original synagogue, dedicated in 1927, was located at 1910 Broadway Avenue in the Beechview neighborhood of the city of Pittsburgh. That building was demolished to make way for a library. Beth El relocated to Mount Lebanon in 1962. *Photograph by Julian H. Preisler, 2013*

Mount Lebanon, Allegheny County—Beth El's original facility on Cochran Road was constructed in 1962 and designed by Carl Pearlman. A new Sanctuary designed by Mr. Pearlman was dedicated in 1967 with additions and expansions to the synagogue campus in 1978 and 1998. Beth El is the repository of artifacts, furniture, and memorial plaques from several closed synagogues in southwest Pennsylvania. *Photograph by Julian H. Preisler, 2013*

Jefferson Hills, Allegheny County—Beth Israel Center is an Independent Conservative congregation established in 1959. The present synagogue at 118 Gill Hall Road was built in 1963, and is located in the South Hills region of Pittsburgh. Many of the original founders were engineers from New York who moved to Pittsburgh for employment at the nearby Westinghouse nuclear lab. *Exterior photograph by Julian H. Preisler, 2013*

Pittsburgh, Allegheny County—Beth Hamedrash Hagadol Beth Jacob is an historic Orthodox congregation established in 1869 as B'nai Israel and chartered in 1873. The Beth Jacob Congregation, also Orthodox, was established as a breakaway from Beth Hamedrash Hagadol in 1883 and in 1964 merged back with the congregation to form the present congregation. The congregation purchased the former Central Blood Bank Building at 810 5th Avenue downtown and reconstructed and renovated it into the present synagogue, which was opened in 2010. *Photograph by Julian H. Preisler, 2013*

Pittsburgh, Allegheny County—Beth Hamedrash Hagadol Beth Jacob was originally located in the Hill District. Their 1892 synagogue on Washington Street was destroyed by fire in 1960. In 1965, they dedicated their modern A-Frame style synagogue at 1230 Colwell Street, also in the Hill District. That synagogue was torn down around 2008 to make way for a new sports arena. *Photograph by Julian H. Preisler, 1995*

Pittsburgh, Allegheny County—The interior of the now demolished Colwell Street synagogue had a beautiful wooden carved Ark, wood pews and massive stained glass windows. All of the artifacts from this building removed and were re-incorporated into the new synagogue on 5$^{th}$ Avenue. *Vintage photograph courtesy of the Rauh Jewish Archive at the Senator John Heinz History Center, Pittsburgh, c. 1965*

Pittsburgh, Allegheny County—Beth Shalom is a historic Conservative congregation located at 5915 Beacon Street in the Squirrel Hill section of the city. Beth Shalom, established in 1917, was one of the first synagogues to relocate from the Hill District. The present synagogue was constructed in 1923 with additions built in 1931 and 1970. After a devastating fire in 1996 that damaged all areas of the synagogue, the complex was restored and rebuilt. *Photograph by Julian H. Preisler, 2013*

Pittsburgh, Allegheny County—B'nai Emunoh Congregation is an Orthodox congregation founded in 1927. The present building at 4315 Murray Avenue in the Squirrel Hill neighborhood was built in 1948. In 2011 Chabad Lubavitch of Pittsburgh was looking for synagogue space and assumed ownership of the building as the present congregation was in decline. It is now known as B'nai Emunoh Chabad. *Photograph by Julian H. Preisler, 1992*

Pittsburgh, Allegheny County—B'nai Israel is a former congregation which was once located in the East End of Pittsburgh. The congregation was established in 1911 and, in 1924, their landmark synagogue at 327 North Negley Avenue was opened. The Byzantine-Revival style synagogue was designed by Henry Hornbostel along with Alexander Sharove. The congregation closed in 1995 due to a decline in the neighborhood Jewish population and merged with Beth Jacob of New Kensington to form Adat Shalom Congregation. *Photograph by Julian H. Preisler, 2013*

Pittsburgh, Allegheny County—B'nai Israel experienced tremendous growth from the time the original synagogue and sanctuary was built in 1924. To accommodate this growth a community center and school addition were built in 1953. When the synagogue closed and relocated to suburban Cheswick, the building was sold. The former community center and school wing are now used as a charter school. *Photograph by Julian H. Preisler, 2013*

Pittsburgh, Allegheny County—The 1953 brick and stone addition was built in the modern style of the time, and materials were used to mirror those used in the original sanctuary. The façade features numerous bas-relief sculptures with Jewish themes. *Photograph by Julian H. Preisler, 2013*

Pittsburgh, Allegheny County—The round sanctuary of B'nai Israel was a massive space with a large dome. It was colorful and richly decorated. Much of the Bimah furniture, artifacts and artwork from the sanctuary were incorporated into Adat Shalom's new synagogue in suburban Cheswick. The Negley Avenue sanctuary is currently empty and in need of some restoration. *Photograph by Hans Jonas and courtesy of Jonas Photography, Pittsburgh, 1997.*

Pittsburgh, Allegheny County—Cneseth Israel Congregation was an Orthodox congregation established in 1905 in the Hill District. That same year a former church on Miller Street was purchased and remodeled for use as a synagogue. The congregation moved to the East Liberty neighborhood in 1946 and, in 1978, Cneseth Israel merged with the nearby Adath Jeshurun congregation. The merged congregation later moved to suburban Monroeville, but closed in 2002. *Photograph courtesy of the Rauh Jewish Archives at the Senator John Heinz History Center, Pittsburgh, c. 1990*

Pittsburgh, Allegheny County—Kether Torah Congregation is an Orthodox congregation established in 1907 as Congregation Anshe Volinia. The congregation became Keser Torah in 1914. Their large domed synagogue at 2043 Webster Avenue in the Hill District was built in 1921. By 1957, the congregation changed its name to Kether Torah and purchased a large residence at 5706 Bartlett Street in the Squirrel Hill section of the city, which they converted for use as a synagogue. The building was closed in 2012, and the congregation now meets at the Hillel Academy. The Webster Avenue synagogue still exists and is now used as a church. *Photograph by Julian H. Preisler, 2013*

Pittsburgh, Allegheny County—Machsikei Hadas was an Orthodox congregation established in 1904. Their synagogue, located at 849 Wylie Avenue in the Hill District of Pittsburgh, was built around 1909 and demolished after 1990. The congregation relocated to the Highland Park neighborhood in Pittsburgh's East End in 1953. *Photograph courtesy of the Rauh Jewish Archive at the Senator John Heinz History Center, Pittsburgh, n.d.*

Pittsburgh, Allegheny County—In 1953, Machsikei Hadas Congregation left the Hill District and rebuilt a residence at 815 North Negley Avenue for use as a synagogue. The congregation disbanded in 1989 due to declining membership and demographic shifts in the neighborhood. *Photograph by Hans Jonas courtesy of Jonas Photography, Pittsburgh, 1989*

Pittsburgh, Allegheny County—The sanctuary interior of Machsikei Hadas reflected old world Orthodoxy and the Bimah, or reader's platform, was placed facing the Ark. The Bimah and other artifacts were donated to the Rauh Jewish Archives when the congregation closed. *Photograph by Hans Jonas courtesy of Jonas Photography, Pittsburgh, 1989*

Pittsburgh, Allegheny County—The New Light Congregation is an unaffiliated Conservative/Egalitarian congregation located at 1700 Beechwood Blvd in the Squirrel Hill neighborhood. The present congregation is a 1912 merger of the original Oher Chodesh, founded in 1899, and the Shaare Shamayim Anshe Romanian Congregation. New Light's original name was Ohel Jacob and was one of several Orthodox congregations with a primarily Romanian Jewish membership. The congregation left the Hill District in 1955 and built their present facility in 1957. *Photograph by Julian H. Preisler, 2013*

Allison Park/McCandless, Allegheny County—Congregation Ohav Shalom is a Reform congregation located in the North Hills area of Pittsburgh. Founded in 1968 as the North Hills Jewish Community Center, the congregation met in various locations until 1979 when a former church on Duncan Avenue in Hampton Township was purchased and remodeled for use as a synagogue. That synagogue was dedicated in 1980. *Vintage image courtesy of Jackie Leicht, Ohav Shalom*

Allison Park/McCandless, Allegheny County—The present contemporary synagogue of Ohav Shalom is actually located in the town of McCandless, though most refer to the location as Allison Park. It was formerly a defunct sports club that was totally remodeled and rebuilt. The new synagogue was dedicated in 1999 and expanded in 2008. Ohav Shalom also has a Holocaust Memorial Sculpture Garden which was the vision of Jack Roseman, a congregant and Holocaust Survivor. The artist was congregant Michael Kraus. *Photograph by Aaron Schmid, 2013*

Allison Park/McCandless, Allegheny County—The Ark and Bimah of Ohav Shalom are contemporary in style. The carved Ark surround and bronze Ark doors are the work of congregant and nationally known sculptor Michael Kraus. The doors are in the shape of the Decalogue or Ten Commandments. The sanctuary has stained glass windows with a theme of the four seasons. *Photograph courtesy of Jackie Leicht, Ohav Shalom, n.d.*

Penn Hills, Allegheny County—The Parkway Jewish Center—Congregation Sha'are HaShamayim is a liberal Egalitarian/Conservative congregation established in 1955 in the eastern suburbs of Pittsburgh. Ground was broken for the present brick and stone synagogue in 1959. The facility was expanded again in 1965 with a religious school and administrative wing. *Photograph by Gail Levine and courtesy of the Parkway Jewish Center, 2013*

Penn Hills, Allegheny County—The religious school children of the Parkway Jewish Center pose in front of their synagogue sometime in the early to mid-1960s. It appears that the addition of 1965 had not yet been built. *Vintage Images courtesy of the Parkway Jewish Center, n.d.*

Pittsburgh, Allegheny County—Poale Zedeck Congregation is a Modern Orthodox congregation located at 6318 Phillips Avenue in the Squirrel Hill neighborhood of Pittsburgh. It was founded in 1881 by Hungarian Jewish immigrants and originally located in the Hill District. The present historic synagogue was dedicated in 1929 and features many colorful terracotta embellishments. A modern school addition, Rabbi Joseph Shapiro Educational Center, faced in light blue panels was built in 1956. The synagogue is a Squirrel Hill landmark and was the first Orthodox synagogue built in the neighborhood. *Photograph by Richard W. Clark, 2013*

Pittsburgh, Allegheny County—The Poale Zedeck synagogue has beautiful stained glass windows throughout the entire building. They are quite ornate and colorful and contain only Jewish symbols and designs and no human figures. *Photograph by Richard W. Clark, 2013*

Pittsburgh, Allegheny County—The sanctuary of the Poale Zedeck synagogue contains a horseshoe shaped women's balcony, an ornate Ark and surround, plus a beautiful light blue dome over the center of the worship space. The light fixture in the dome is quite intricate and features eight seven-branched menorahs. *Photograph by Richard W. Clark, 2013*

Pittsburgh, Allegheny County—Rodef Shalom Congregation is Pittsburgh's first, and traces its origins to 1847, when a Jewish burial society was established. This was the first Jewish organization of any kind in the city. The present historic synagogue at 4905 Fifth Avenue was designed by the noted Pittsburgh architect Henry Hornbostel and completed in 1907. It is of yellow brick with colorful terracotta embellishments. A religious school, auditorium and chapel were added in the 1930s. The Biblical Botanical Garden, the largest in North America, was added in 1986/1987. Renovations and restorations to the historic Sanctuary and other parts of the complex were done between 1989 and 2003. *Photograph by Julian H. Preisler, 2013*

Pittsburgh, Allegheny County—Rodef Shalom expanded over the years as the congregation grew and additional facilities were needed. In addition to what was added on in the 1930s, a large social hall was added in 1956. Design and decorative elements on this building were done in a way to compliment the historic sanctuary of the synagogue complex. *Photograph by Julian H. Preisler, 2012*

Pittsburgh, Allegheny County—Rodef Shalom needed to expand to accommodate growth, but chose to remain on the site where the original synagogue was located. The Eighth Street synagogue was demolished in 1900 and a new synagogue with ornate rose window was dedicated in 1901. With additional growth, this new synagogue became inadequate only three years later in 1904. The new, but inadequate synagogue was sold to Second Presbyterian Church, and the congregation purchased land at Fifth and Morewood Avenues in Oakland. *Vintage image courtesy of the Rauh Jewish Archives of the Senator John Heinz History Center, Pittsburgh, n.d.*

Pittsburgh, Allegheny County—Rodef Shalom's 1907 sanctuary is an enormous space with an octagonal stained glass skylight in the dome, elegant Mahogany woodwork, a large choir and organ loft. William Willett designed the stained glass windows and the lighting features the seven-branched menorah. *Vintage image courtesy of Martha Berg and the Rodef Shalom Archives, c. 1908*

Pittsburgh, Allegheny County—In 1902, Beth Tzedek Congregation was formed by Russian Jewish immigrants. It was also known as Beth Israel. A splinter group formed Beth David in 1905 and began construction on their synagogue at 23 Miller Street in the Hill District. Unable to complete construction, the splinter group reunited with Beth Tzedek to form Shaare Tefilah in 1906, and construction was completed on the new synagogue. Around 1947, the congregation relocated from the Hill District to Squirrel Hill. Due to declining membership, the congregation disbanded in the mid-1990s. The former Miller Street synagogue is one of the few remaining former synagogues in the Hill District. *Photograph by Julian H. Preisler, 2013*

Pittsburgh, Allegheny County—Shaare Torah Congregation is an Orthodox congregation located at 2319 Murray Avenue in the Squirrel Hill neighborhood. Established in 1880 by Jewish immigrants from Lithuania, the congregation built its first synagogue at 35 Townsend Avenue in 1909 in the Hill District. The congregation left the Hill District in 1944 and dedicated the present brick and stone synagogue in 1948. It is one of Squirrel Hill's largest Orthodox congregations. *Photograph by Julian H. Preisler, 2013*

Pittsburgh, Allegheny County—The entrance to Shaare Torah features bas-relief Judaic sculptures and the symbols of the Twelve Tribes of Israel. The sanctuary features windows of stained glass and was recently remodeled. *Photograph by Julian H. Preisler, 2013*

Pittsburgh, Allegheny County—Talmud Torah Congregation is a former synagogue, also known as the Sarah Street Shul, located at 1908 Sarah Street on Pittsburgh's South Side. The Orthodox congregation was founded in 1914, and the synagogue was dedicated in 1917. By 1970 the congregation had disbanded due to a lack of members in the area. The present structure is now an apartment building. *Photograph by Julian H. Preisler, 2013*

Mount Lebanon, Allegheny County—Temple Emanuel of South Hills is a large Reform congregation located in Mount Lebanon in Pittsburgh's South Hills. It was established in 1951 to serve the growing number of Jewish families moving to the area. The original synagogue was constructed between 1953 and 1960. Renovations and expansions took place between 1990 and 2003 to expand the synagogue campus. Temple Emanuel also has a Holocaust Memorial Garden. *Photograph by Julian H. Preisler, 2013*

Mount Lebanon, Allegheny County—The initial building of Temple Emanuel was built in two stages. The first floor was completed in 1954. In 1960 the sanctuary and social hall were added. It was designed by the renowned synagogue architect Percival Goodman. It is a large beige and brown brick structure with numerous stained glass windows and a roof that sweeps upward. *Photograph by Julian H. Preisler, 1995*

Mount Lebanon, Allegheny County—The chapel, or Beit HaT'fila, at Temple Emanuel was dedicated in 2003 and was part of an extensive expansion designed by congregation member Dan Rothschild. It is decorated in muted colors of white and light yellow. The Ark is a contemporary piece of artwork done in metal. *Photograph by Saralouise Reis and courtesy of Temple Emanuel, 2013*

Pittsburgh, Allegheny County—Temple Sinai is a large Reform congregation chartered in 1946 as Pittsburgh's second Reform synagogue. The Worthington Mansion at 5505 Forbes Avenue in the Squirrel Hill neighborhood was purchased in 1947 for use as the synagogue. The property next door to the mansion was purchased in 1955 for expansion, and in 1957 a religious school and auditorium were built there. The present modern Sanctuary was dedicated in 1969. *Photograph by Julian H. Preisler, 2012*

Pittsburgh, Allegheny County—The 1969 Leebov Sanctuary was built to blend with and complement the adjacent Worthington Mansion of Temple Sinai. The contemporary style space contains modern stained glass windows set within numerous angled windows. *Photograph by Julian H. Preisler, 2012*

Pittsburgh, Allegheny County—The interior of temple Sinai's circular sanctuary features a contemporary Ark, Eternal Light, and stained glass window above the Ark. The space was completely renovated in 2005. *Photograph by John Schiller and courtesy of Temple Sinai, 2013*

Pittsburgh, Allegheny County—Torath Chaim Congregation was an Orthodox congregation established in 1927. Their former synagogue is located at 728 North Negley Avenue in the East Liberty neighborhood. The residence that served as the synagogue was extensively remodeled in 1931 and again in 1948 with the addition of a large mural and a women's balcony. Due to declining membership numbers and population shifts, the congregation closed in 2004. It was the last remaining Jewish congregation in Pittsburgh's East End. *Photograph by Julian H. Preisler, 2013*

Pittsburgh, Allegheny County—Tree of Life Or L'Simcha is a Conservative congregation located at 5898 Wilkins Avenue in the Squirrel Hill neighborhood. It was established in 1864 and chartered in 1865 as Etz Hayyim by former members of Rodef Shalom. In 1882, the congregation purchased a church building and began using the name Tree of Life. In 1886, the congregation joined the Conservative movement. Their first purpose-built synagogue on Craft Avenue was dedicated in 1907. In 1946 the congregation relocated to Squirrel Hill. The Hailperin Sanctuary was dedicated in 1963 and features modern stained glass windows. In 2010, Congregation Or L'Simcha (f. 2007 by members of Beth Shalom) merged with Tree of Life to form the present congregation. Dor Hadash, Pittsburgh's Reconstructionist congregation (f. 1963) also meets at this synagogue. *Photograph by Julian H. Preisler, 2013*

Pittsburgh, Allegheny County—The Tree of Life Congregation's original Squirrel Hill synagogue is a stone and brick building constructed between 1946 and 1953. The land was donated by then synagogue president, Charles J. Rosenbloom, and the cornerstone was made of limestone from Palestine. As the congregation grew, the original building was connected to the new sanctuary. This "bridge" building features a large tree of life sculpture on the exterior. *Vintage image courtesy of the Rauh Jewish Archive of the Senator John Heinz History Center, Pittsburgh, c. 1970*

Pittsburgh, Allegheny County—The cornerstone of the Craft Avenue synagogue of the Tree of Life Congregation was laid in 1906 and, when completed in 1907, it had seating for 750 people. When the congregation moved to Squirrel Hill, their synagogue was purchased by the Pittsburgh Playhouse and has served as their home ever since. It is the best maintained of the former synagogues in the Hill District. *Photograph by Julian H. Preisler, 2012*

Punxsutawney, Jefferson County—Chevra Agudas Achim was an Orthodox congregation organized and chartered in 1886. The cornerstone of the first synagogue was laid in September 1900, and the synagogue was dedicated in December of that year. The original synagogue was demolished to make way for a new bridge project, and a modern synagogue was built in 1949 on Church Street. When the congregation closed in the early 1980s, the memorial plaques were moved to the synagogue in DuBois. The local historical society was given some of the congregation's artifacts. The building is now an accounting office. The Punxsutawney Jewish Cemetery is located in nearby Cloe. *Photograph by Julian H. Preisler, 2013*

Punxsutawney, Jefferson County—Chevra Agudas Achim's last building was a small, simple building, but it was the face of the Punxsutawney Jewish community that had existed since 1886. It stands as a reminder that Jews once lived and flourished in town. *Photograph by Julian H. Preisler, 2013*

Punxsutawney, Jefferson County—The cornerstones from the old and new synagogues of the Chevra Agudas Achim Congregation can still be found on the building. They are the only remaining clue to the former use of the building. The colored glass windows in the former sanctuary also remain. *Photograph by Julian H. Preisler, 2013*

Rochester, Beaver County—The Tree of Life Congregation was established in 1927, though Jewish worship services were held as early as 1918. The synagogue at 390 Pinney Street was built in 1928 and is now home to the Hancock Architecture firm. By 1973, the synagogue closed due to a decline in the local Jewish population, and its assets were turned over to the now closed Beaver Valley United Jewish Community in Beaver Falls. *Photograph by Julian H. Preisler, 2013*

Sharon, Mercer County—Beth Israel was a Reform congregation originally established as Orthodox in 1888 and chartered in 1902. They built their first synagogue on Shenango Street in 1903 and expanded it in 1924. The congregation later became Conservative and, by 1949, had joined the Reform movement. In 1950, a new synagogue, designed by Youngstown architect Morris Scheibel, was built at 840 Highland Road. Synagogues in the adjacent city of Farrell, B'nai Zion (f. 1901) and Ahavath Achim (f. 1916), eventually merged with Beth Israel. The Farrell synagogues are no longer extant. In 2013, Beth Israel closed the synagogue and merged with the Reform Rodef Sholom Congregation in Youngstown, Ohio. Stained glass windows and artifacts will be transferred to their new home. The synagogue's Holocaust Memorial will be moved to the Jewish Community Center in Youngstown and the Sharon building will be put up for sale. *Photograph by Julian H. Preisler, 1996*

Sharon, Mercer County—The sanctuary of Beth Israel in Sharon featured an elegant Ark, light colors, and many stained glass windows. On a personal note, the author's cousin, Rabbi Jacques Cukierkorn, once served as the Rabbi for Beth Israel in Sharon. The Jewish cemeteries for the community are located in the adjacent city of Farrell. *Photograph by Julian H. Preisler, 1996*

Tarentum, Allegheny County—Ohev Scholom Congregation was an Orthodox (later Conservative) congregation established in 1900. Their synagogue was built in 1923 and closed in 1973 due to a decline in the local Jewish population. Most members joined the Beth Jacob Congregation in nearby New Kensington, and the proceeds of the sale of the synagogue were given to Beth Jacob. Beth Jacob later merged with B'nai Israel of Pittsburgh to form Adat Shalom. The former synagogue in Tarentum is now used as an apartment building. *Photograph by Julian H. Preisler, 2010*

Titusville, Crawford County—B'nai Gemiluth Chesed Congregation was an Orthodox congregation chartered in 1870. Their first synagogue was built at Martin and Waters Street. It was replaced in 1875 or 1880 by a new synagogue at Martin and Walnut Streets. The synagogue was still active in the 1950s, but disbanded in the mid-1970s. The building was used for a variety of purposes and then fell into disrepair. It was demolished sometime after 2009. Titusville is famous for the discovery of oil in the vicinity in 1859 and the launching of the modern petroleum industry. *Vintage image courtesy of the Rauh Jewish Archives at the Senator John Heinz History Center, Pittsburgh. n.d.*

Titusville, Crawford County—B'nai Zion was a Reform congregation established prior to 1872 by German Jewish families. The synagogue at 318 North Franklin Street was built in 1872 and closed around 1890. The building is now the home of a graphics/printing company. Many of the original stained glass windows have been restored, and the building has been repainted to accent its unique architecture. It serves as the only reminder to a vanished Jewish community. *Photograph courtesy of Bruce Pratt, n.d.*

Uniontown, Fayette County—Temple Israel is a former Reform synagogue located at 119 East Fayette Street. The impressive Neo-Classical style synagogue was built in 1908 at a cost of $25,000, just four years after the congregation was organized in 1904. Temple Israel sold their ornate temple and relocated to space in the Uniontown Jewish Community Center before 2000. The congregation was closed in 2012 and the last function of the congregation was a Bat Mitzvah celebration. *Photograph by Julian H. Preisler, 2013*

Uniontown, Fayette County—The Tree of Life Synagogue was organized as an Orthodox congregation in 1902. The present building on Pennsylvania Avenue was dedicated in 1925. The congregation later became Conservative and then Reform. The congregation put their synagogue up for sale in 2013 and made plans to move to the Uniontown Jewish Community Center. There are two Jewish cemeteries in nearby Hopwood, one for each congregation in Uniontown. They are the Hebrew Cemetery Association (Temple Israel) and the Jewish Holy Society Cemetery (Tree of Life Congregation). *Photograph by Julian H. Preisler, 2013*

Uniontown, Fayette County—The Tree of Life synagogue is a brown and beige brick building with a round stained glass window featuring a Star of David above the entrance. A Star of David design is also featured just above the door to the synagogue. The sanctuary also features a number of stained glass windows and a balcony. *Photograph by Julian H. Preisler, 2013*

Warren, Warren County—Tephereth Israel Congregation was an Orthodox synagogue located at 112 Conewango Avenue. The congregation was organized in 1904 and disbanded in 1994 due to a decline in the local Jewish population. The synagogue, which was originally built as a church in 1918, was sold to a local church in 1996. Tephereth Israel was also known as the Warren Hebrew Congregation. *Photograph courtesy of Lawrence R. Lawson of Temple Beth El in Bradford*

Washington, Washington County—Congregation Beth Israel is a Conservative congregation formed in 1891 and chartered in 1901. The congregation used a variety of locations for services until they built their first synagogue in 1902 at a cost of $4,500. The present synagogue at 265 North Avenue was dedicated in 1955 and designed by Alexander Sharove, who designed a number of synagogues in western Pennsylvania. Beth Israel is now the only active synagogue in Washington County. *Photograph by Marilyn Posner and courtesy of Beth Israel, 2013.*

Washington, Washington County—Beth Israel's original building at North Franklin and West Spruce Streets still stands, but has been altered quite a bit over the years and is no longer recognizable as a former Jewish house of worship. It is currently used by the Knights of Columbus. *Photograph by Marilyn Posner and courtesy of Beth Israel Congregation, 2013*

Washington, Washington County—An old sketch shows how the original Beth Israel in Washington looked when it was a Jewish house of worship. It was a simple brick structure with stained glass windows on the façade, including a round window with a Star of David. *Sketch courtesy of Beth Israel Congregation, n.d.*

White Oak, Allegheny County—Temple B'nai Israel is a Reform congregation formed in 1912 in nearby McKeesport. The congregation was originally Conservative. In 2000, Temple B'nai Israel purchased the former synagogue of the Tree of Life Sfard Congregation in White Oak. Tree of Life Sfard was previously located in McKeesport and chartered in 1898 as a merger of the Sfard Anshe Galicia and Tree of Life congregations. Their White Oak synagogue was built in 1975. *Photograph courtesy of Temple B'nai Israel, n.d.*

White Oak, Allegheny County—The Gemilas Chesed Congregation has been located in White Oak since 1963 when their new synagogue was dedicated. The downstairs sanctuary contains the Ark, Bima and pews from their old 1904 synagogue in McKeesport which was demolished in 1963. The main sanctuary contains large colored glass windows that compliment the mid-century style of the synagogue. *Photograph by Julian H. Preisler, 2012*

Not to be forgotten are several Pittsburgh synagogues, photographs of which could not be included in this book because of space limitations. Pittsburgh has many historic and large synagogues, but there were also a number of smaller congregations that were located in converted residences or shared space in Jewish communal buildings and schools. They were located mostly in the Hill District, Oakland, the North Side and Squirrel Hill. Most of these "Old World" style Orthodox congregations are no more, but a few still remain active. Beth Abraham Congregation was formed in 1888 and became mostly a burial and cemetery association by the mid-1940s; Tiphereth Israel Congregation was organized around 1890 and lasted into the 1940s; Congregation Shaare Zedek was established in 1895 and merged with the Young Israel Congregation in 1974; Beth Israel Congregation was established in 1907 and closed sometime after 1948; Ohave Zedeck Synagogue was active from its founding in 1917 until the 1970s; Adath Israel Congregation was established in 1923 and closed in 1993; Chofetz Chaim Congregation existed from 1925 to about 1972; Other former congregations include Beth Mogan David established around 1908, Kneseth Israel formed in 1910, Anshe Libovitz begun in 1907; Ahavath Zedeck formed in 1908, Beth Jehuda dating from 1913, Kehilath Jeshurun from 1930, and Lawrenceville's Butler Street Congregation formed in 1905. The Young People's Synagogue in Squirrel Hill is an active havurah-style congregation established in 1946. It merged with the B'nai Zion Congregation (f. 1921) in 1996. The congregation and is also known in Hebrew as Bohnai Yisrael.

# Bibliography

*The Beth Samuel Jewish Center 75$^{th}$ Anniversary* (Ambridge, PA, Beth Samuel Jewish Center, 1985)

*Beth Yehuda Dedication Book* (Lock Haven, PA, Beth Yehuda Synagogue, 1952)

Bronner, S. J., *Greater Harrisburg's Jewish Community* (Charleston, Arcadia Publishing, 2010)

Chernofsky E., *Traveling Jewish In America* (Lodi, NJ, Wandering You Press, 1991)

Feldman, J. S., *The Jewish Experience in Western Pennsylvania: A History 1755-1945* (Pittsburgh, Historical Society of Western Pennsylvania, 1986)

*A Guide to Historic Landmarks in Beaver County, Pennsylvania*, Charles Townsend, Bob Bauder & Denver Walton.

Israelowitz, O., *Guide to Jewish Canada & USA: Volume 1—Eastern Provinces* (Brooklyn, O. Israelowitz, 1990)

Israelowitz, O., *Guide to Jewish USA, Volume 1 The Northeast* (Brooklyn, O. Israelowitz, 1987)

*Jewish Congregations & Synagogues: Pittsburgh, Pennsylvania* (Pittsburgh, Rauh Jewish Archives Heinz History Center, n.d.)

Koppman, L & Postal, B., *American Jewish Landmarks: A Travel Guide and History—Volume 1 The Northeast* (New York, Fleet Press Corporation, 1977)

Koppman, L & Postal, B., *A Jewish Tourist's Guide To The U.S.* (Philadelphia, The Jewish Publication Society of America, 1954)

*Pittsburgh Tri-State Pinkas* (Pittsburgh, Pittsburgh Jewish National Fund Council, 1949)

Preisler, J. H., *American Synagogues: A Photographic Journey* (Falling Waters, WV, Julian H. Preisler, 2008)

Shevitz, A. H., *Jewish Communities on the Ohio River: A History* (Lexington, KY, The University Press of Kentucky, 2007)

*125$^{th}$ Anniversary Journal 1866-1991* (Williamsport, PA, Temple Beth Ha-Shalom, 1991)

Many synagogue and historical websites were very helpful to my research. The website "JewishGen KehilaLinks" was very useful and introduced me to the Jewish history in Brownsville, Canonsburg, Greensburg, Lewistown, McKeesport, Monessen and Uniontown.

# Glossary Of Hebrew Names

Adas also Adath Israel—Community of Israel also Congregation of Israel

Adat Shalom—Community also Congregation of Peace

Ahavath also Ahavas Achim—Brotherly Love

Ahavath Sholom—Love of Peace

Agudath Achim also Agudas Achim—Association of Brothers

Anshe Chesed—People of Loving-Kindness

Anshe Hadas—People of Renewal

Beit HaT'fila—House of Prayer

Beth Am also Ahm—House of the People

Beth David—House of David

Beth El—House of G-d

Beth Ha-Shalom—House of the Peace

Beth Israel—House of Israel

Beth Jacob—House of Jacob

Beth Jehuda—House of Judah or Tribe of Judah

Beth Samuel—House of Samuel

Beth Shalom and Beth Sholom—House of Peace

Beth Tikvah—House of Hope

Beth Tzedeck—House of Righteousness

Bimah, Bema—the raised platform usually at the front of the sanctuary with the Ark, pulpit, etc.

B'nai Abraham—Sons of Abraham

B'nai B'rith—Sons of the Covenant

B'nai Gemiluth Chesed—Sons of Deeds of Kindness

B'nai Israel—Sons of Israel

B'nai Jacob—Sons of Jacob

B'nai Levi—Sons of Levi

Bohnai Yisrael—Builders of Israel

Brit Shalom also Brith Sholom—Covenant of Peace

Chesed Shel Emeth—Loving-Kindness and Truth

Chevra Agudas Achim—Community Society of Brothers

Chevra Sholom—Association also Community of Peace

Chisuk Emuna—Strengtheners of Faith

Chofetz Chaim—Seeker of Life

Dor Hadash—New Generation

Emanuel and Emanu-El—G-d is with us

Etz Chaim also Eitz Chayim—Tree of Life

Gemilas Chesed Anshe Ungarn—Deeds of Kindness Men of Hungary

Hadar Israel—Fruits of Israel

Havurah—religious fellowship

Kesher Israel—Connection to Israel also Bridge to Israel

Knesseth also Keneseth Israel—Assembly of Israel

Machzikey Hadas also Machsikei, Machsikey—Defenders of the Faith

Ohel Jacob—Tent of Jacob

Oher also Or Chodesch—New Light

Ohave Israel also Ohev, Oheb, Ohav Israel—Lovers of Israel

Ohev/Oheb/Ohav/Ohave Shalom—Lovers of Peace

Ohave Zedeck—Lovers of Justice

Or L'Simcha—Light and Joy also Gladness

Poale Zedeck—Workers of Righteousness

Rodef Shalom also Rodeph Shalom—Pursuers of Peace

Sfard Anshe Galicia—Hassidic Men of Galicia

Shalom, Sholom, Scholem—Peace

Sha'are HaShamayim—Gates of the Heavens

Shaare Shamayim Anshe Romanian Congregation—Gates of Heaven People of Romania

Shaare Tefilah—Gates of Prayer

Shaare Torah—Gates of Learning/Wisdom

Shaare Zedek—Gates of Justice

Talmud Torah—Religious School

Tifereth/Tefares/Tefereth Israel—Splendor of Israel also Glory of Israel

Torath Chaim—Bible of Life